Schools Council
Research Studies

Physical Education
in Secondary Schools

The report of the Schools Council Enquiry
into Physical Education in Secondary Schools,
based at St Mary's College of Education,
Twickenham (1970-1)

Schools Council
Research Studies

Physical Education in Secondary Schools

J. E. Kane

Macmillan Education

© Schools Council Publications 1974

First published 1974
Reprinted 1975

SBN 333 15720 6

Published by
MACMILLAN EDUCATION LTD
Basingstoke and London

Associated companies and representatives
throughout the world

Printed in Great Britain by
Hazell Watson & Viney Ltd
Aylesbury, Bucks

Foreword

The Physical Education Subject Committee of the Schools Council decided, soon after it was established, to publish a statement on the aims and objectives of physical education and to invite discussion of them. The many and varied responses to this statement indicated that there was no clear picture of the place of physical education in the curricula of secondary schools. The Committee realised that it would be difficult to embark upon curriculum development until clarification had taken place. It proposed, therefore, a survey of the place of physical education in secondary schools. The Schools Council approved and made resources available. The survey was directed by Dr J. E. Kane assisted by Miss June Layson, and was carried out during the school year 1970–71.

They survey was intended to provide the basis for a curriculum development project. The Schools Council has accepted the need for such a project and the details are currently being worked out. Meanwhile, however, the Director's report of the survey, published here, not only provides a basis for curricular development by any organisation or by individuals concerned with physical education but also contains many findings which, without further development, are of great significance for teachers in schools.

The Physical Education Subject Committee wishes to express its thanks to Dr Kane and Miss Layson for the thoroughness and competence of the enquiry which they carried out within the terms of reference they were given.

P. C. MCINTOSH
Chairman, Schools Council Physical
Education Subject Committee

Contents

Appendices

Tables and figures

Tables

Appendices

Figures

Acknowledgements

I should like to thank all the physical education teachers and head teachers who co-operated so well to make this enquiry possible. The questionnaire completion and the interviews took a great deal of time and the high rate of response is a tribute to their professional concern.

I take particular pleasure in recording my fullest appreciation of the contribution made by my co-worker, June Layson, who was concerned with all phases of the enquiry and conducted all the interviews.

Christopher Murray gave a great deal of advice on the structuring of the questionnaires, carried out the computing under great pressure, and in general gave all kinds of expert advice. My sincere thanks are willingly given.

I am indebted to Brian Ashley for his work with the sample of independent boys' schools which he describes in Appendix E.

Finally, I wish to thank Mrs E. Forest for numerous tasks of organisation and administration, including the typing of the report in the shortest possible time.

1 Introduction

This report arises from an enquiry into physical education in secondary schools commissioned by the Schools Council and undertaken during the academic year 1970–71. The general purpose of the enquiry was to investigate the circumstances under which physical education forms part of the secondary school programme in England and Wales. The intention was to provide up-to-date information about current practices and trends in physical education curricula as an essential first stage in planning a curriculum development project. In particular the aims of this investigation and enquiry were:

(a) to discover the facts about the place and the programme of physical education in secondary schools;

(b) to consider how far present practices were related to the aims of physical education published in the first issue of the Schools Council newsletter *Dialogue* (September 1968);

(c) to provide information about existing practices to those concerned with physical education;

(d) to use the information as a basis for a future curriculum development project.

These aims were set out in an internal Schools Council paper proposing the enquiry, which was prepared in April 1969 by the Secondary Working Party of the Council's Physical Education Committee.

The enquiry's terms of reference involved the construction of a question-naire for the purpose of ascertaining the factual information required, which was to be collected from a large stratified random sample of schools. Typical items on which information was required were:

(a) the degree of compulsion to take part in some form of physical education at different stages in the secondary school course;

(b) period allocation for physical education in school timetables;

(c) the introduction and range of options;

(d) out-of-school activities;

(e) staffing and facilities;

(f) the criteria by which the physical education curriculum is constructed.

The sample

A one-in-ten random sample of secondary schools in England and Wales was drawn according to the following four-way stratification:

(a) *Type of school:* modern, grammar (maintained and direct grant), technical and other, comprehensive (junior, senior, other), independent;

(b) *Sex of school:* boys, girls, mixed;

(c) *Region:* Registrar-General's divisions—North, York and Humber, North West, East Midlands, West Midlands, East Anglia, Greater London, other South East, South West, Wales;

(d) *Size of school:* up to 300, 301–400, 401–600, 601–800, over 800.

The sample, which identified 575 schools, was prepared with the invaluable help of the Department of Education and Science computer services.

The questionnaire

In the proposal for the enquiry it was recommended that the data should be collected by mailed questionnaire. With the time and resources available this approach was considered to be the most suitable. In effect the questionnaire had to be discussed, constructed, revised, piloted, analysed, adapted, printed and despatched in about ten weeks. The processes involved in the preparation and administration of the questionnaire are dealt with under five headings:

initial stages—interviews and research;
questionnaire construction;
piloting;
identifying the schools and despatching questionnaires;
returns.

INITIAL STAGES—INTERVIEWS AND RESEARCH

It was considered most important in the early stages of the questionnaire construction to interview a number of teachers, in order to have their views on the relevance of the topics to be investigated, and on the most satisfactory way of obtaining the required information. A survey of the related literature was also regarded as a vital preliminary.

Efforts were made to interview a sub-sample of teachers, reflecting the main sample stratification. In the event only teachers in the Midlands and South East were interviewed, but these were considered to be representative of school type and size. Altogether twenty-four physical education teachers and two physical education organisers were interviewed. In addition, discussions took place with several men's, women's and mixed physical education departments, and with a group of teachers taking an in-service course at a college of physical education. Where permission was granted, the interviews were tape-recorded.

Initially interviews were carefully structured, the interviewer having pre-pared specific questions on the selected topics, as recommended by the April 1969 paper. Although this method elicited the desired factual responses on aspects such as physical education facilities and timetable allocation, it was evident that other important information concerning, for instance, teachers' perceptions of their roles, aims and objectives, and their attitudes to content, method and so on, were not forthcoming. Therefore the formal interview was abandoned in favour of free-wheeling discussions in which the interviewer guided the conversation from a semi-structured schedule, but encouraged the teachers to develop pertinent and interesting points and to add their own comments about the enquiry.

It became clear from the interviews that information on the allocation of physical education in the school timetable would best be gained from the head teacher or deputy head. It became evident also that while much informa-tion on other aspects could be given by the heads of physical education departments, in order to tap the whole spectrum of physical education opinion it would be necessary to contact all physical education teachers in each of the schools identified in the sample. Therefore the decision was made to structure and circulate the questionnaire in three parts (see Appendix A):

Part 1: to be completed by the head teacher;
Part 2: to be completed by the head of the physical education department;
Part 3: to be completed by every full-time member of staff teaching physical education.

In particular the interviews provided valuable information on six main issues:

degree of compulsion;
period allocation of physical education in school timetables;
the introduction and range of options;
out-of-school activities;
staffing and facilities;
physical education curriculum criteria.

Degree of compulsion

It was evident that the term 'compulsion' had different interpretations within the physical education context. This led to the formulation of the terms 'compulsory activities', 'compulsory activities with choice', and 'optional activities', which were used and defined in Part II of the questionnaire (see Q.5, p. 70).

Period allocation in school timetables

Not only was it clear from the interviews that this information could best be gained from the head teacher or his deputy, but it was also clear that figures on physical education allocation unrelated to other subjects would be meaning-less. It was decided therefore to compare the time given to physical education with that given to English, mathematics, geography and history in each year group (see Part I, Q.11, p. 65). It was noted from the interviews that important variables such as the variation in physical education allocation for forms in the same year group, the length of a period or lesson, and different timetable cycles would have to be considered in developing a comparative formula. From these considerations the formula for 'average class time' (ACT) was developed:

$$ACT = \frac{\text{combined total of periods in a 5-day cycle for forms within a year}}{\text{number of forms in a year}} \times \text{length of single period}$$

The ACT would seem to be a useful comparative index which is applicable irrespective of pupil choice or size of class, both of which might otherwise be complicating variables in any general assessment of time allocation.

The introduction and range of options
The notion of 'options' was interpreted very differently by many teachers and this contributed to the decision described under 'degree of compulsion' above. Furthermore, the synonymous use of 'options' and 'activities' in many cases indicated the need to ascertain exactly what is taught in the name of physical education in schools. From the divergence of teachers' views expressed in this area, it was obvious that the actual content of the physical education programme should be investigated (see Part II, Q.3, p. 68).

Out-of-school activities
This phrase was also found to have different connotations for teachers. From the material provided by the interviews, four elements of the term 'extra-curricular activities' emerged, identified as:

time of day(s) involved;
duration;
activities taken;
membership patterns.

This area was of undoubted interest and concern to all teachers, and therefore was placed in Part III of the questionnaire (see Qs 18–21, pp. 79–80).

Staffing and facilities
From the interviews, particularly those with heads of departments, this topic appeared both important and complex. 'Staffing' (including qualified and unqualified coaches) and 'physical education teaching policy' were identified as Qs 2 and 10 in Part II (see pp. 67 and 73), but the teachers' comments on facilities indicated several difficulties. It seemed that a listing of physical education facilities would be feasible but of limited value. The perception of the adequacy of facilities in relation to the physical education programme was regarded as of much greater importance. Therefore, questions on the adequacy

of facilities both on and off the school site were devised and, since all the teachers interviewed attached considerable importance to one or more of the perceived concomitant factors, questions on changing, showering, and travelling were included in Part II (see Qs 6–9, pp. 71–3).

Physical education curriculum criteria
The very wide divergence of opinion evident from the interviews clearly indicated that questions on aims and objectives should be included in Part III.

SURVEY OF LITERATURE FOR PERTINENT INFORMATION
This survey was specifically concerned with two areas:

    physical education activities;
    aims and objectives.

Physical education activities
An intensive search through a considerable range of literature produced evidence to show that at least sixty activities can be said to form part of the physical education programme in secondary schools in England and Wales. The list was reduced to a more manageable one of thirty-five on the basis of common occurrence for the purposes of Q.3 in Part II (see pp. 68–9).

    Physical education literature was also the starting point for the attempt to characterise or group physical education activities so that information could be gained about the emphasis placed upon the different activities at various times in the physical education programme. This work led to the formation of Q.4 in Part II (see p. 69).

Aims and objectives
Starting with the aims and objectives stated in *Dialogue 1*, an intensive search of both British and American literature was undertaken in order to assemble all relevant information on programme objectives. A frequency check was taken and the nine approaches most often referred to in the literature were listed. Efforts were made to identify these objectives in a manner that could be presented to the teacher in an unequivocal format. The results of this exercise form the basis of Q.15 in Part III (see pp. 76–7).

QUESTIONNAIRE CONSTRUCTION
Having partially structured Parts I, II, and III of the questionnaire in outline, further interviews and discussions were undertaken to devise supporting questions and to ensure that the questionnaire would cover adequately all those aspects which would contribute to the fullest information on physical education in the secondary schools.

    Thus in Part I questions to describe the particular school 'profile' were posed, including two which gave information on which a simple socioeconomic index could be constructed. It was thought that these indices might be used as variables in cross-tabulations and analyses. Questions on the school immigrant population and streaming were also included, since it was considered that these might have an important bearing on the school programme.

Part II was structured to gain factual information from the head of department concerning the syllabus, emphasis, policy and facilities.

Part III was assembled to secure the individual teacher's reactions to certain important issues central to his function as a physical education teacher. Biographical details were sought in the first group of questions, and these were followed by questions concerning their opinions, attitudes, teaching styles and involvement in extra-curricular activities. A final section was constructed so as to gain teachers' views on 'pupil effects', 'influencing factors', and 'teacher characteristics'.

PILOTING

The three-part questionnaire was completed and despatched to a pilot sample consisting of thirty-three schools from the Birmingham conurbation and seven from Middlesex and Surrey. Care was taken to ensure that the pilot sample generally reflected as far as possible the categories of type, sex and size of the schools to be used in the main sample.

The response rate to the pilot questionnaire was 83% (i.e. thirty-three schools replied out of forty), a good return considering that schools had less than two weeks in which to complete and return the questionnaire. The piloting stage proved invaluable in three respects:

(a) information was gained on the profitability of asking questions in certain areas;
(b) the actual wording of the questionnaire was subject to teacher scrutiny;
(c) many teachers took the opportunity to add comments which were generally helpful.

As a result the questionnaire was reconstructed in those areas where ambiguity, overlap and inconsistency were indicated. Because the main questionnaire was due to be posted to schools before the end of the autumn term 1970, it was not possible to re-pilot the amended questionnaire.

IDENTIFYING SCHOOLS AND DESPATCHING QUESTIONNAIRES

The 575 schools in the sample were identified with the assistance of the DES computer staff and officers of the Schools Council. Permission was quickly given by 128 LEAs for the enquiry to proceed, and subsequently the two other LEAs concerned gave their permission. Estimates were made of the number of physical education teachers in each school and packages of the appropriate number of questionnaires were assembled and despatched on 30 November 1970.

RETURNS

The letter accompanying the questionnaire asked for completion and return as soon as possible and preferably by the end of term. Despite the shortage of time and pressures associated with end of term activities, most schools were able to return the questionnaire before the Christmas vacation, while others returned their questionnaires during the vacation or at the beginning of the spring term.

Table 1.1 Distribution and return of questionnaires

	No. of schools
Sample	
One-in-ten sample drawn	575
School closures, amalgamations, etc.	−6
LEAs withholding permission	−1
Working total	568
Returns	
Completed questionnaires	468
Letters	11

As shown in Table 1.1, completed returns were received from 468 of the 568 schools in the sample. This represents an 82% return index. Of the eleven letters received in lieu of the questionnaire returns:

(a) three schools could not, for various reasons, complete the questionnaire by the suggested date but indicated that they would make a return as soon as organisational changes had been arranged;

(b) four schools declined to co-operate, stating that organisational changes prevented a clear picture of physical education being given;

(c) two schools did not have physical education in their curriculum;

(d) one school had yet to appoint physical education staff;

(e) one public school found the questionnaire not applicable to its circumstances.

There is little doubt that the prolonged postal strike which was in operation at the time accounted for many non-returns. In addition, because of the strike it was not possible to embark upon normal follow-up procedures. In these circumstances, the percentage of returns must be considered satisfactory.

2 Data preparation and analyses

The data

The three parts of the questionnaire taken together contained some 264 items. Item responses were precoded wherever appropriate. Some opportunity was given in open-ended questions and other ways for respondents to provide additional information, which has been collated and introduced at relevant points in this report. This allowed respondents to elaborate beyond the limits set by the questionnaire and to offer their opinion of the items.

After the scoring, marking, and calculations had been completed, the data were assembled on punched cards. For each of the three parts of the questionnaire the data fitted conveniently on two eighty-column cards. In all more than 4000 cards of data were initially prepared.

Analyses

In general the investigation was regarded as a broad survey, and for the most part therefore a basic descriptive statistical approach was utilised. For all items the total sample means, standard deviations and percentages were computed. In addition, these statistics were computed and tabulated separately for a number of sub-samples, e.g. for men and women teachers and for types of school. The cross-tabulations undertaken (mostly comparing items by sex or school type) were chosen, within the limits set by the resources available, for their obvious and immediate interest, but many other tabulations and basic analyses of this data would be rewarding and may be undertaken when time and additional resources permit.

Although the primary intention was to prepare a basic descriptive survey of the data, it was not possible to resist attempting a somewhat more elaborate analysis of information supplied in Part III on, for example, pupil effects, influencing factors and teacher characteristics. In addition to ranking the responses to the items in 22–4, three component analyses were computed to see if it were possible to identify a small number of factors (i.e. groupings of items), which might be used to describe teachers' reactions.

Almost all the computations were carried out on the University of London computer. In particular the XTAB, BMD07D, and Fortap programs were used.

3 Average class time

The common assumption that a decreasing amount of time is allocated to physical education over the secondary years is supported by the evidence in this analysis. An index of average class time was used to compare the time given to physical education with that given to English, mathematics, geography and history. Whereas the average time allocated to these subjects was shown to be greater in the fifth year than in the first year, a substantial and consistent decrease in time for physical education was demonstrated. For none of the secondary years did physical education time compare favourably with the time given to English and mathematics, but for the first four years physical education had a substantially greater allocation than geography or history. While the biggest increase in time for the four academic subjects during the first five years was between the fourth and fifth years, it was between these years that the greatest decrease occurred for physical education. Sixth form time given to physical education showed no decrease on what was allocated in the fifth form, but compared much less favourably with the other subjects than in the earlier years.

When the analysis was extended to compare physical education time for grammar, secondary modern and comprehensive schools, the grammar schools appeared to have the greatest overall time allocation, secondary modern schools experienced the biggest fifth year decrease, and comprehensive schools allocated least time to physical education over the first five years of secondary schooling.

★   ★   ★

The average class time (ACT) for five curriculum subjects—English, mathematics, geography, history, and physical education—in a five-day timetable cycle for each school year (see Part I, Q.11, pp. 65–6) was computed according to the formula mentioned earlier:

$$\text{ACT} = \frac{\begin{array}{c}\text{combined total of periods in}\\ \text{a 5-day cycle for forms within a year}\end{array}}{\text{number of forms in a year}} \times \text{length of single period.}$$

Appropriate adjustments were made for the small number of schools whose timetables ranged from $5\frac{1}{2}$-day to 10-day cycles.

The ACT for any curriculum subject calculated in this way gives a general index of the school's weekly commitment to that subject for a particular year group. The ACT for a curriculum subject may, more specifically, be interpreted as the average time in one week that a pupil may spend on the subject. There are, of course, a number of variables in the time allocation to a subject of which the ACT is not, and was not intended to be, a sensitive index. These include the time allocated to different forms, seasonal differences in time allocation, and the size of the class taking the subject.

The curriculum subjects English, mathematics, geography, and history, which were chosen to provide a comparison with physical education, were thought to include both those which are regarded as the most highly emphasised in our education system (English and mathematics) and those which are popularly considered to be less emphasised (history and geography). No doubt the inclusion of a wider range of curriculum subjects in this section of the investigation would have been much more rewarding. Even for the subjects chosen, however, the calculations and computations involved were time-consuming and tedious.

The ACT for the schools in the sample on five curriculum subjects over the seven years of secondary schooling is reported in Table 3.1. Means and standard deviations are given for 422 schools over the first five years, and for 224 schools over the two sixth form years. The standard deviation may be interpreted as a measure of the spread of the scores—the higher the standard deviation, the greater the spread or dispersion of scores. The distribution of the mean scores is also presented for convenience in histogram form (Fig. 1). Because the curriculum for the sixth form years is normally structured in quite a different manner from that of the early secondary years, especially in providing for choice and specialism, the analyses for these years are considered separately.

Secondary years 1–5

The data in Table 3.1, which are illustrated in Fig. 1, provide a comparison between the five curriculum subjects over the years of secondary schooling. For the first five years the general picture is that English, mathematics, geography and history show an increase in the time allocated to them as measured by the ACT index while physical education (including games) shows a considerable decrease of almost one-third. The other general observation is that there appears to be much in common between scores for English and mathematics and between those for history and geography.

Table 3.1   ACT (minutes per week) for five subjects over the seven secondary years ($n = 422$ schools for years 1–5, 224 schools for years 6–7)

Year		English	Mathematics	Geography	History	PE
1	Mean	218·5	200·0	92·5	92·4	152·6
	SD*	46·7	31·2	37·6	37·5	42·4
2	Mean	210·3	195·5	90·6	89·8	144·6
	SD	46·1	31·7	28·0	27·6	40·1
3	Mean	204·7	191·6	92·2	90·8	135·6
	SD	41·5	29·7	23·8	22·6	38·3
4	Mean	202·3	192·6	120·4	118·5	125·2
	SD	40·8	30·4	37·6	38·1	45·1
5	Mean	218·8	204·6	145·1	143·0	104·5
	SD	53·9	46·5	38·4	38·4	47·1
6	Mean	255·6	274·3	235·9	239·7	108·7
	SD	60·7	84·9	69·6	66·7	58·5
7	Mean	266·5	293·2	259·3	261·6	104·4
	SD	73·5	85·3	58·0	57·5	44·7

* Standard deviation.

The amount of time allocated to both English and mathematics is high compared with the other three subjects, and the pattern of variation over the five years is similar for these two subjects. An even more striking agreement may be seen between the mean scores for geography and history.

English mean scores are the highest for each of the five years. The average allocation in the first year is 218·5 minutes (almost equivalent to five 45-minute lessons), and a slight drop is recorded over the following three years. In the fifth year the mean allocation rises to approximately the same level as in the first year. The mathematics mean scores are the second highest in each of the five years and over these years show the smallest variation. Starting with a mean score of 200 minutes in the first year (equivalent to five 40-minute lessons), there is a slight drop for the following three years before recovery to a mean score of 204·6 minutes.

Geography and history have very similar mean scores over the five years. They occupy the lowest two places in the ranking of the five subjects over the first four years. However, for both subjects a substantial and similar increase in allocated time is shown in the fourth and fifth years. The fifth year mean

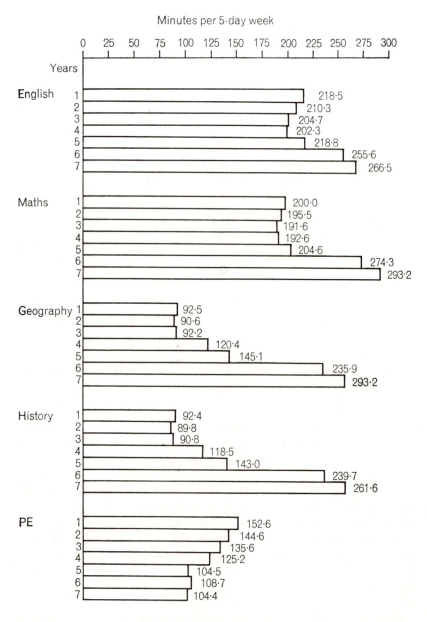

Fig. 1 Mean scores for ACT in five subjects for all types of school combined (*n* = 422 schools for years 1–5, 224 for years 6–7)

scores for geography and history represent an increase of more than 50% on their first year scores. This increase reflects no doubt the introduction of options in the fourth and fifth years as a consequence of which some pupils spend more time on selected subjects.

Physical education time varies considerably over the five years and the pattern of variation is in clear contrast to that for the other four subjects. The mean score in the first year of 152·6 minutes (equivalent to just less than four 40-minute lessons), represents a much bigger allocation than for history or geography. In each of the following four years the average time for physical education decreases by larger amounts until in the fifth year the average time for this subject is 104·5 minutes. Of the five subjects under review, this is the only one where such a trend is reported.

Some notion of the relative allocation of total time given to the five subjects over the five-year period may be gained by comparing the sum of the five mean scores for each subject. On this basis English has the highest overall allocation followed closely by mathematics; physical education comes next with approximately three-fifths of the time given to English; and geography and history, with almost identical scores, get least time with approximately half the time given to English.

An inspection of the standard deviations shows that geography, history and mathematics have the lowest spread of scores, indicating a relatively higher level of agreement between schools on the amount of time given to these subjects. Physical education scores, in contrast, are very widely dispersed, reflecting a great deal of variation in the allocation of time by different schools. It is, however, the secondary modern schools, of which there were 195 in the sample, that account for the largest variation. The standard deviations for this group of schools (Table 3.2, p. 15) were found to be considerably higher in each year than for any other group.

Sixth form years

Not all the schools in the sample had sixth form classes, so the mean scores shown in Table 3.1 for the sixth and seventh years are computed for only 224 schools. Only one in five of the secondary modern schools, for instance, was able to complete sixth form returns.

The ACT for the sixth and seventh years requires a different interpretation from that for the earlier years. English, mathematics, geography and history are subjects chosen by some but not all students, and because students tend to specialise in a small number of subjects the amount of time allocated to each is, and needs to be, much greater than before. Consequently the ACT computed for the sixth form years will be expected to show higher mean scores on the four academic subjects. There will be a tendency too for the ACT in each of these subjects to be an index of the total time commitment of different groups of students. As might be expected for sixth form academic subjects, the time allocation for each is not found to be greatly dissimilar. Mathematics and English, in that order, are still however found to have a somewhat higher ACT than history and geography. The increase of time in the seventh year over the sixth is also according to expectation. It will be noted that the standard deviations for sixth form scores are very high, suggesting a great deal of variation between schools.

The ACT for physical education in the sixth and seventh years approximates to that found for the fifth year, which is perhaps not in accord with the common assumption that less time is given to this subject in the sixth form. Of course, the meaning of the sixth form ACT is somewhat different from that for the fifth year. There is an almost universal application of the notion of student choice for physical education in sixth forms, by which students may or may not choose to avail themselves of the time and opportunities offered by the school. Therefore the amount of time allocated to physical education and represented by ACT must generally be regarded as available time which may or may not be used. The ACT in this case must be read more as the school's commitment and less as the total student impact that physical education makes. The question of the degree of compulsion to participate is discussed in some detail in Chapter 4.

ACT for physical education according to type of school

An analysis of the ACT for physical education according to type of school was considered to be a worthwhile extension of the investigation. The main sample comprised eight types of school in varying numbers:

grammar, maintained	82
grammar, direct grant	16
secondary modern	195
comprehensive	89
junior high	11
senior high	5
independent	18
technical	6

A comparison between maintained grammar, secondary modern and comprehensive schools appeared to be the most realistic because of the relatively large number of schools in each category. Table 3.2 gives the means and standard deviations of the average class time for physical education in these three groups of schools for each of the seven years of secondary schooling. The means for the total sample of schools are included for comparison. Fig. 2 (p. 16) represents the mean scores in histogram form.

The general pattern of a decreasing amount of time for physical education over the years of secondary schooling is evident for each of the three types of

Table 3.2 Comparative analysis of ACT (minutes per week) in PE for grammar maintained, secondary modern and comprehensive schools

Year		Grammar maintained	Secondary modern	Comprehensive	Total sample
		$n = 82$	$n = 195$	$n = 89$	$n = 422$
1	Mean	157·5	151·4	141·3	152·6
	SD	39·3	42·5	33·6	39·3
2	Mean	142·7	143·5	136·0	144·6
	SD	35·0	39·9	33·0	40·1
3	Mean	129·8	135·7	129·6	135·6
	SD	31·1	38·0	29·3	38·3
4	Mean	119·1	125·3	116·7	125·2
	SD	26·2	41·0	31·1	45·1
5	Mean	110·7	91·0 ($n = 171$)	105·3	104·5
	SD	26·7	37·6	30·9	47·7
		$n = 82$	($n = 39$)	$n = 50$	$n = 224$
6	Mean	108·0	99·1	95·0	108·7
	SD	44·3	43·3	40·9	58·5
7	Mean	107·3	86·0 ($n = 15$)	95·3	104·4
	SD	44·0	28·0	38·0	44·7

school. There are, however, some differences between the three profiles which are of interest.

In the first year the grammar schools' average allocation (157·5 minutes) is the highest for the three groups of schools, and is significantly above that for the total sample, but in the second, third and fourth years it falls increasingly below this index. In the fifth year the grammar schools' mean of 110·7 minutes is again the highest of the three school groups and again is significantly above the mean for the total sample. Taking the total of the weekly mean allocation over the first five years, the grammar schools (659·8 minutes) have about 2% more time over this period for physical education than secondary modern schools (649·9), and a significant 5% more than comprehensive schools (628·9). The greater allocation of time for physical education in grammar schools is much more obvious for the two sixth-form years, where on average they get 16% and 13% more time than secondary modern and comprehensive schools respectively.

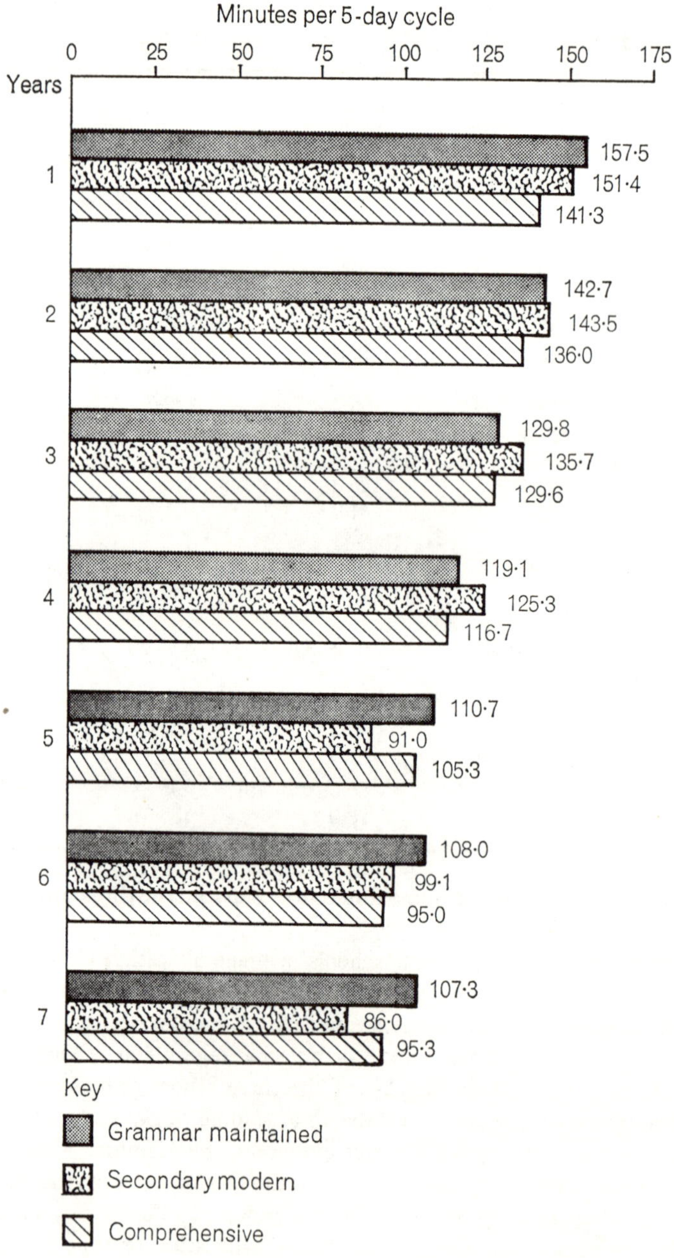

Minutes per 5-day cycle

Fig. 2 Comparison of mean scores for ACT in physical education for three types of school

The mean for the secondary modern group of schools for the first four years approximates to the total sample mean, and in the second, third and fourth years is the highest of the three groups. The fifth year mean is notable in that it represents a considerable decrease in time (approaching one standard deviation) from the fourth year allocation. This fifth year mean is computed on a reduced number of schools ($n = 171$) since not all the secondary modern schools in this sample had a fifth year. It might be assumed that in schools with a fifth year the orientation during this year would be towards the preparation for various examinations. Examination pressure might in some way be a factor contributing to the greatly reduced allocation of time to physical education in this fifth year. However, the teasing out of such a complex relationship is outside the scope of this investigation and no evidence is available here on which a cause-and-effect relationship may be imputed. Thirty-nine of this group of schools had a sixth year and there were fifteen only with a seventh year. The mean time given to physical education in both these sixth form years was relatively very low.

Only in the fifth year does the ACT score for the comprehensive schools approach the total sample mean. For all the other six years the mean time allocated is much lower. Although the largest decrease is seen to be from year four to year five, as with the secondary modern schools, the difference is relatively less significant.

4 The teachers

This chapter outlines the findings of the enquiry with regard to biographical details of the teachers and certain aspects of their professional work setting. The physical education wing of the teaching profession was found to be very young on average and to be almost entirely non-graduate. The men tended to teach another subject and to be more ambitious for further qualifications than the women. In the majority of cases the physical education teacher was the only one in his or her department, and 83% of all departments surveyed had no more than two full-time staff. There was, however, evidence that physical education departments had a great deal of part-time and occasional help from other teachers and from coaches. The full-time physical education teachers undertook, in addition to their normal curricular commitments, extra-curricular duties with their pupils; for most teachers these were estimated to take between six and nine hours per week. The influences which the teachers feel have the greatest effect on their work are described as total work commitment, diversity of pupils and resources. They consider that the most important characteristics for the successful physical education teacher are personal education, social concern and ability to establish rapport.

★ ★ ★

In Part II and Part III of the questionnaire questions were asked about the teachers' background and training, about the time they spent with their pupils outside the curriculum, about the factors which they thought influenced their work as teachers, and about the personal characteristics which they considered important for the successful teacher to have. The findings on these items give a biographical and a professional profile of the teachers in the sample.

Biographical details

Of the 888 returns 433 (48·7%) were from women teachers and 455 from men.

Age
The average age of the total sample was just under twenty-six years. The average age for men is just over twenty-six years, and for women twenty-five years. The percentage distribution of men and women in the various age groups is summarised in Table 4.1.

Table 4.1   Age of teachers

Age group	Men ($n = 455$)	Women ($n = 433$)
21–22 years	8%	19%
23–25	28%	38%
26–30	23%	19%
31–39	29%	14%
40 and over	12%	10%

Marital status
Respondents were asked to indicate their marital status and whether or not they had children. Table 4.2 summarises the results for men and women in percentages.

Table 4.2   Marital status of teachers

Status	Men ($n = 455$)	Women ($n = 433$)
Single	27%	51%
Married without children	24%	36%
Married with child(ren)	39%	13%

Length of teaching service
Table 4.3 illustrates length-of-service patterns among men and women physical education teachers, again by percentages.

Table 4.3   Length of teaching service

Service (years)	Men ($n = 455$)	Women ($n = 433$)
Less than 1	10%	14%
1–3	27%	35%
4–6	18%	20%
7–9	13%	10%
10–12	13%	5%
13–15	6%	7%
Over 15	13%	9%

Specialist teacher qualifications
Question 10 in Part III of the questionnaire (see p. 76) attempted to distinguish in a general manner between different methods of gaining a specialist teacher qualification in physical education. The results for men and women are summarised in Table 4.4.

Table 4.4   Specialist teacher qualifications

Qualifications	Men ($n = 453$)	Women ($n = 430$)
Third-year supplementary one-year course	23%	6%
Three-year continuous course	63%	83%
One-year course for graduates	2%	0%
Other	12%	11%

Previous employment
Almost 22% of all teachers in the sample ($n = 888$) had been employed full-time in another profession or occupation prior to becoming a teacher. Table 4.5 gives further details of previous employment.

Table 4.5   Previous employment

Time spent in previous employment	Men ($n = 455$)	Women ($n = 433$)
None	66%	91%
Less than 1 year	10%	3%
1–5 years	18%	5%
6–10 years	4%	1%
Over 10 years	2%	0%

Teaching subjects other than physical education
Of the total sample of 888 teachers, 58% reported that they were regularly teaching one or more subjects in addition to physical education. The analysis for men and women teachers is given in Table 4.6.

Table 4.6   Extent of specialisation

Subjects taught	Men ($n = 455$)	Women ($n = 433$)
Physical education and other subject(s)	70%	44%
Physical education only	30%	56%

Graduate qualifications
Almost 4% of the total sample of 888 teachers of physical education were graduates. A further analysis revealed that 6% of men, but only 2% of women, had a degree.

GCE A-level qualifications
Almost 43% of the men and 39% of the women had no A-level qualifications but the remainder of the men and women had passed on average in two subjects.

Plans for further qualifications
With regard to their aspirations towards gaining additional qualifications, 45% of the men and 80% of the women had no immediate plans for further study. Those who had plans were distributed as shown in Table 4.7.

Table 4.7 Plans for further qualifications

Projected qualifications	Men ($n = 250$)	Women ($n = 86$)
B.Ed.	30%	42%
B.A./B.Sc.	27%	16%
Advanced Diploma in a specialisation	33%	31%
M.A./M.Phil., etc.	7%	7%
Ph.D.	3%	4%

Staffing

Question 2 in Part II of the questionnaire (see p. 67) asked for the number and type of teachers who contributed to the physical education programme. Returns were made on behalf of 340 boys' departments and 333 girls' departments. The findings are summarised in Tables 4.8–4.14.

It will be noted that 4% of departments had the assistance of nine or more other teachers. One school with a roll of over 2000 pupils and over 200 staff

Table 4.8 Number of full-time PE teachers

Full-time teachers	PE depts ($n = 673$)
0	10·0%
1	56·2%
2	27·0%
3	5·85%
4	0·80%
5	0·15%

indicated that 100 members of staff were involved in timetabled physical education.

Table 4.9 Number of part-time PE teachers

Part-time teachers	PE depts ($n = 673$)
0	65%
1	26%
2	7%
3	1%
4	1%

Table 4.10 Number of other members of staff who assist with timetabled PE

Teachers assisting with timetabled physical education	PE depts ($n = 673$)
0	39%
1	16%
2	14%
3	10%
4	6%
5	3%
6	3%
7	2%
8	3%
9 and over	4%

Table 4.11 Number of other members of staff who assist with extra-curricular PE

Teachers assisting with extra-curricular physical education	PE depts ($n = 673$)
0	36%
1	20%
2	11%
3	8%
4	7%
5	5%
6	3%
7	2%
8	2%
9	6%

Table 4.12 Number of qualified coaches/instructors (unqualified teachers) who assist with timetabled PE

Coaches assisting with timetabled physical education	PE depts ($n = 673$)
0	75%
1	16%
2	5%
3	2%
4	0·5%
5	1%
6	0·5%

Table 4.13 Number of qualified coaches/instructors (unqualified teachers) who assist with extra-curricular PE

Coaches assisting with extra-curricular physical education	PE depts ($n = 673$)
0	84%
1	11%
2	3%
3	1%
4	0%
5	0%
6	1%

The above information on staffing shows that more than one-third of the departments (33·8%) have two or more full-time physical education teachers, but it is somewhat surprising to find that there are 10% of schools without any physical education teachers committed to teach physical education full-time. It is interesting to note the number of other teachers and coaches/instructors who play an apparently large part in the timetabled and extra-curricular programmes of physical education. The nature of the contribution that these other teachers and coaches make is currently subject to serious discussion. As one teacher put it during the preliminary interview:

I feel that one of the most important issues that will face the profession in the next few years is that with such a wide field of activities now being presented in many schools, can one teacher—the 'PE specialist'—be expected to teach each activity to a reasonably high standard? In other words, will the part-time coach or expert in a specialised field become increasingly prominent in our larger schools?

Extra-curricular duties

Teachers were asked to give information about their extra-curricular activities, which were defined as 'those activities outside the normal timetable in which physical education teachers are often involved as part of their work'. They were requested to indicate the times when they were regularly involved in this extra-curricular work, to estimate the time they gave to these duties, to give information about the specific activities with which they were regularly concerned, and to specify the conditions for pupil membership of the extra-curricular groups.

Time devoted to extra-curricular activities
Of the total sample of 888 physical education teachers who answered the questionnaire, 87% said they were involved in lunch-time activities, 94% were involved in after-school activities (immediately after school and evening), 74% were regularly engaged in Saturday morning activities, and 5% worked regularly before the school day began.

From comments added to the questionnaire it was clear that there was a considerable difference between the time given to extra-curricular activities by men and that given by women. The percentage distribution of time spent on extra-curricular activities is shown in Table 4.14. It can be seen that slightly less than a third of the men and slightly more than a third of the women gave 6–9 hours per week to this extra work. Almost another third of the women gave more than nine hours per week, and more than 50% of the men estimated that they fell into this category. In their written comments some teachers suggested that remuneration should be made for those hours of additional work.

Table 4.14 Number of hours per week spent on extra-curricular duties

Hours	Men ($n = 455$)	Women ($n = 429$)
Less than 1	2·9%	7·0%
3–6	14·5%	29·0%
6–9	28·6%	34·0%
9–12	24·2%	20·0%
12–15	18·7%	5·8%
15–18	7·2%	3·8%
18–21	2·8%	0·2%
Over 21	1·1%	0·2%

Types of activity
Table 4.15 shows the results of a question asking teachers to indicate the types of extra-curricular activities in which they are regularly involved.

Table 4.15 Proportion of teachers involved in each extra-curricular activity (n = 832)

Teachers involved in each activity	Type of activity
98%	Team games
73%	Athletics
49%	Gymnastics
36%	Swimming
31%	Outdoor pursuits
17%	Dance
39%	Other

It can be seen that nearly all teachers involved in extra-curricular activities regularly teach or coach team games. In addition, nearly 40% reported that they are involved in activities other than those specifically listed.

Membership criteria

Teachers were asked to give the membership criteria for their extra-curricular activities—whether membership was open, partially selective (at the discretion of the teacher) or according to ability. For each type of membership a five-point rating scale for the number of activities involved was used, a rating of 5 indicating that all activities were included, and a rating of 1 indicating that no activities fell into the particular membership category (see Q.21, p. 80). A score of 3 represented the mid-point. Table 4.16 gives the findings for men and women for each of the three membership categories.

Table 4.16 Use of membership criteria for extra-curricular activities

Membership category	Men (n = 442) Mean	SD	Women (n = 415) Mean	SD
Open	3·10	1·3	3·14	1·3
Ability-based	2·62	1·3	2·56	1·2
Partially selective	2·18	1·5	2·46	1·2

It can be seen that there is considerable similarity between the means obtained for men and women. Open membership is apparently the rule for about half the activities (means of 3·10 and 3·14) taught or coached. Membership on ability is rated somewhat lower, and selection according to the teacher's discretion has relevance in only a few activities offered in extra-curricular time, with mean scores of 2·18 for men teachers and 2·46 for women.

Influencing factors

Question 23 of Part III (see pp. 83–4) set down twenty items which might, to different extents, affect the teachers in carrying out their perceived role. The teachers were asked to rate each item on a five-point scale from 'very important' (1) to 'not at all important' (5). A zero return was allowed where teachers were 'not sure' about rating the item according to its influence in their school work. Means, standard deviations and n (reflecting zero) returns were calculated for each item and are shown in Table 4.17. A 'not sure' response was omitted from the calculations and the n for the item reduced accordingly. A high n for an item ($n = 852$) indicates that relatively few respondents were 'not sure'. The rankings shown in this table are based on the mean ratings.

Table 4.17 Teachers' assessment of the importance of factors influencing their work ($n = 852$)

Influencing factor	V. important				Not at all important	Not sure	Mean	SD	n	Rank
	1	2	3	4	5	0	Mean	SD	n	Rank
(1) Timetabled teaching load	1	2	3	4	5	0	2·0	1·1	800	6
(2) Extent of help afforded by non-PE staff	1	2	3	4	5	0	2·2	1·3	835	7
(3) Special demands made on physical education teacher because of his/her expertise (injuries, first aid, sports day, etc.)	1	2	3	4	5	0	2·6	1·3	837	10=
(4) Diversity of curricular activities	1	2	3	4	5	0	2·3	1·1	810	8=
(5) Attitude of school staff to physical education	1	2	3	4	5	0	1·9	1·1	850	5
(6) Adequacy of facilities available for physical education	1	2	3	4	5	0	1·4	0·7	850	1
(7) Recognition from superiors of worthwhile work	1	2	3	4	5	0	2·3	1·2	842	8=

Table 4.17—*cont.*

Influencing factor	V. important 1	2	3	4	Not at all important 5	Not sure 0	Mean	SD	n	Rank
(8) Freedom given to the teacher to experiment with different instructional approaches	1	2	3	4	5	0	1·6	0·9	845	2=
(9) Extra duties assigned during the school holidays	1	2	3	4	5	0	2·8	1·3	832	15=
(10) Number of clerical duties which have to be discharged	1	2	3	4	5	0	2·8	1·3	833	15=
(11) A considerable proportion of pupils hostile to 'school'	1	2	3	4	5	0	3·0	1·3	827	18=
(12) Legal liability for accidents	1	2	3	4	5	0	2·9	1·4	826	17
(13) Total number of different pupils who have to be taught	1	2	3	4	5	0	2·6	1·4	839	10=
(14) 'Intellectually inferior' label sometimes associated with physical education	1	2	3	4	5	0	3·6	1·5	830	20
(15) Difficulty for some pupils in providing required equipment*	1	2	3	4	5	0	3·0	1·3	839	18=
(16) Amount of money allotted to physical education for equipment	1	2	3	4	5	0	1·6	0·9	847	2=
(17) Problem of 'discipline' in the special physical education situation	1	2	3	4	5	0	2·7	1·4	829	12=
(18) Inequitable use of shared facilities	1	2	3	4	5	0	2·7	1·4	787	12=
(19) Timetable allocation given to physical education	1	2	3	4	5	0	1·6	0·9	849	2=
(20) Range of individual abilities within classes	1	2	3	4	5	0	2·7	1·4	849	12=

* e.g. a tennis racquet.

Table 4.18 Highest ranked influences

Rank	Influence	Item
1	Adequacy of facilities	6
2 =	Timetable allocation to PE	19
2 =	Amount of money allocated	16
2 =	Freedom to experiment	8
5	Attitude of school staff to PE	5
6	Timetabled load	1

Table 4.19 Lowest ranked influences

Rank	Influence	Item
15 =	Number of clerical duties	10
15 =	Extra duties assigned	9
17	Legal liability for accidents	12
18 =	Difficulty for pupils in providing equipment	15
18 =	Pupils hostile to 'school'	11
20	'Intellectually inferior' label	14

The six items considered the most important as influences are ranked in Table 4.18, and the six rated lowest in Table 4.19.

Comparing the six highest ranked items with the six lowest ranked, it was clear that there were considerably smaller differences of opinion and greater certainty among teachers in their rating of the former. This interpretation is based on the lower standard deviations and higher n returns for the higher ranked items (see Table 4.17).

With a view to giving a more parsimonious description of these items from the teachers' responses a factor analysis was undertaken which produced seven components. These factors, which describe the main underlying structure of the items and the way in which the items cluster together, are

Table 4.20 Influences: major factors

Factor
(i)   Total work commitment
(ii) Diversity of pupils
(iii) Resources
(iv) Liberal atmosphere
(v)   Safety
(vi) Attitude of colleagues
(vii) Discipline

listed in order of importance and size in Table 4.20. The full details of the analysis are given in Appendix C, pp. 98–100.

The largest factor, *total work commitment*, describes both the formal curriculum load and the extra duties expected of physical education teachers. The second factor, *diversity of pupils*, reflects both the range of pupils' abilities and the number of different classes taught. The third factor, *resources*, takes in items referring to the adequacy of equipment, staffing and timetable. The other factors are smaller and less complex; their names reflect the interaction of the major items which they comprise.

Scores on each of the first three factors or elements—total work commitment, diversity of pupils, and resources—were obtained from each teacher. Then a comparison was made between the mean scores for:

(*a*) men and women teachers;
(*b*) the five age groups of the teachers (see Q.4, p. 75).

The details of these analyses are also given in Appendix C (pp. 100–3).

When the mean scores for men and women on total work commitment and diversity of pupils were compared, no significant difference was found, but on the third factor, resources, women had a significantly higher mean. Apparently women teachers of physical education, compared with their male colleagues, consider that the resources available have a greater influence on their work.

The mean scores for the five age groups on the three factors were also considered for possible differences. Again on total work commitment and diversity of pupils, no differences were found, but on resources the youngest teachers were more convinced than others that resources affect their work (see Appendix C, p. 102).

Teacher characteristics

In Part III, question 24, teachers were asked to consider and rate twenty-four personal characteristics for successful physical education teaching.*

As with question 23, each characteristic could be rated on a five-point scale and a rating of zero was allowed for respondents who were 'not sure' about rating an item. The mean rating, standard deviation and *n* for each item are shown in Table 4.21. Where zero was recorded, no rating was included in the calculation but a reduction in *n* for the item was noted. As in Table 4.17, therefore, *n* is an index of the certainty of teachers about the relevance of the item.

* The items listed in the question (see pp. 85-6) were based on those prepared by Professor D. S. Anderson, of the Australian National University, Canberra. Acknowledgement must also be made to Dr. G. W. Miller, of the Department of Higher Education, University of London Institute of Education, for his help with this section of the report.

Table 4.21   Teachers' assessment of the importance of certain teacher characteristics (n = 852 overall)

Characteristic	V. important			Not at all important	Not sure	Mean	SD	n	Rank
	1	2	3	4	5	0			
(1) Being able to communicate ideas	1	2	3	4	5	0	1·2	0·4	849	2
(2) High standards of honesty and integrity	1	2	3	4	5	0	1·4	0·8	845	5
(3) A thorough knowledge of the subject-matter	1	2	3	4	5	0	1·3	0·6	851	3=
(4) A capacity for meticulous attention to details	1	2	3	4	5	0	2·6	1·0	843	18
(5) Extroverted personality	1	2	3	4	5	0	2·8	1·2	829	19
(6) A capacity for sustained hard work	1	2	3	4	5	0	1·5	0·8	851	6
(7) Creative ability	1	2	3	4	5	0	2·1	1·0	840	16
(8) Maturity of outlook	1	2	3	4	5	0	1·9	0·9	835	12=
(9) A desire to improve the world or society in some way	1	2	3	4	5	0	3·3	1·3	831	23
(10) A pleasing manner and appearance	1	2	3	4	5	0	1·7	0·9	852	7=
(11) Well spoken and well dressed	1	2	3	4	5	0	2·0	1·0	851	14=
(12) Ability to gain the respect and confidence of pupils with whom the teacher deals	1	2	3	4	5	0	1·1	0·3	852	1
(13) Having contacts within teaching profession	1	2	3	4	5	0	3·1	1·3	828	21=
(14) Ability to get on well with colleagues	1	2	3	4	5	0	1·8	0·9	850	10=
(15) Ability to inspire confidence	1	2	3	4	5	0	1·3	0·5	851	3=
(16) A concern for the interests and well-being of the community	1	2	3	4	5	0	2·4	1·1	845	17
(17) A family background in teaching	1	2	3	4	5	0	4·8	0·5	842	24
(18) A broad cultural knowledge	1	2	3	4	5	0	3·0	1·1	845	20
(19) Administrative ability	1	2	3	4	5	0	1·7	0·9	850	7=
(20) A good academic record	1	2	3	4	5	0	3·1	1·0	846	21=

Table 4.21—*cont.*

Characteristic	V. important				Not at all important	Not sure	Mean	SD	n	Rank
	1	2	3	4	5	0				
(21) A knowledge of recent developments in educational practice	1	2	3	4	5	0	1·9	0·9	852	12=
(22) A knowledge of child psychology	1	2	3	4	5	0	2·0	0·9	848	14=
(23) Interest in social background of pupils	1	2	3	4	5	0	1·8	0·9	849	10=
(24) Belief in equality of opportunity for everybody	1	2	3	4	5	0	1·7	0·9	845	7=

The six items considered most important as characteristics of the successful teacher are ranked in Table 4.22; the rankings between these six items represent only a slight difference of opinion.

Table 4.22 Highest ranked teacher characteristics

Rank	Characteristics	Item
1	Ability to gain respect and confidence of pupils	12
2	Being able to communicate ideas	1
3=	Ability to inspire confidence	15
3=	Thorough knowledge of subject-matter	3
5	High standards of honesty and integrity	2
6	Capacity for sustained hard work	6

The items occupying the lowest six places of the twenty-four are shown with their rankings in Table 4.23. Except in the case of item 17, which is generally adjudged to be of negligible importance, the ranking of the items in this table represents only slight differences of opinion.

In general it may be seen that teachers were more certain (higher *n*) and differed least (small standard deviation) on the six highest ranked items. Most uncertainty and difference of opinion was recorded for the lower ranked items 13, 9 and 5. Against this general trend is the lowest ranked item, family background in teaching, about which there is almost no disagreement.

Table 4.23 Lowest ranked teacher characteristics

Rank	Characteristic	Item
19	Extroverted personality	5
20	Broad cultural knowledge	18
21=	Good academic record	20
21=	Contacts within teaching profession	13
23	Desire to improve world or society	9
24	Family background in teaching	17

Dr G. W. Miller* used a similar list of teacher characteristics and asked college of education students to judge the importance of each. His students also included items 12, 1, 15 and 2 in their highest ranked six. Knowledge of subject matter (item 3) and capacity for sustained hard work (item 6) were much lower rated by the students than by the teachers. Of the lowest six items rated in the present study, four of them were likewise found in Miller's lowest six. Family background in teaching was also found by him to be clearly the lowest rated item, even though 15% of his sample had a parent who was a teacher.

Table 4.24 Teacher characteristics: major factors

Factor	Items
(i) Personal education	20, 18, 21
(ii) Social concern	9, 16, 8
(iii) Rapport	12, 1, 15
(iv) Knowledge of children	22, 23, 24
(v) Professional organisation	19, 14, 13
(vi) Assurance	5, 17, 11
(vii) Application	4, 3, 6

A factor analysis based on the intercorrelations between the teachers' scores on the twenty-four items was undertaken to identify the underlying factors or elements. This showed that the items which were scored in a similar way clustered together into seven major factors. The factors were described after an inspection of the items which accounted for them (for details, see Appendix C, pp. 103–5), and are listed in order of importance and size in Table 4.24.

The largest factor, *personal education,* is a broad-based factor having sub-

* A.T.O. *Enquiry: Students Becoming Teachers* (University of London Institute of Education, 1971).

stantial links with eight items only, the biggest three of which are shown in Table 4.24; the factor emphasises all-round education—professional, cultural and academic. The second factor, *social concern*, covers concern for others and society at large. The third factor, *rapport*, is concerned with ability to gain respect and develop confidence and good interpersonal relationships. Factor four refers to general *knowledge of children*, psychological, social and educational. The fifth factor, *professional organisation*, emphasises administrative ability and necessary professional links. Factor six links items which together describe a disposition of *assurance*, and the final factor, *application*, involves the grouping of items referring especially to the teacher's need for meticulous attention to detail (item 4) and his capacity for sustained hard work (item 6).

The first three factors, personal education, social concern and rapport, were used as sub-scales and scores on each were calculated for the individual teachers. Further analyses were then undertaken to compare the mean scores on these three factor scales for:

(*a*) men and women;
(*b*) the five age groups of the teachers (see Q.4, p. 75).

The details of these analyses are reported in Appendix C, pp. 105–7.

No significant differences were found between the mean scores for men and women teachers on these three major dimensions, which were considered by both men and women specialist teachers to be important characteristics for successful physical education teaching.

However, when the scores were compared according to the age groups of the teachers, the three analyses revealed significant differences. In each case a general trend with age was found, in which the youngest teachers rated personal education, social concern and rapport significantly higher than older teachers (see Appendix C, pp. 107–8).

5 The curriculum

In this chapter, information has been assembled about some factors that are important in the planning and operation of the curriculum in physical education. An attempt has been made to consider evidence from the enquiry which presents teachers' reactions to aspects of the curriculum process. These range from the identification and rating of objectives, through the consideration of such modifying factors as facilities, content, teaching styles and opportunities for the pupils' choice, to the perceived effects of the physical education programme on the pupils.

★   ★   ★

These interrelated aspects of the present physical education curriculum are considered in the following order:

(a) objectives;
(b) facilities;
(c) programme activities;
(d) activity emphasis;
(e) teaching styles and gymnastics approach;
(f) departmental policy;
(g) degree of compulsion;
(h) pupil effects.

Objectives

Question 15 of Part III (see pp. 76–7) listed and briefly described nine objectives that are regularly found in the literature of physical education. These nine objectives were the ones most often mentioned in a review of over 200 publications. The teachers were asked to rank these objectives from 1 (highest) to 9 (lowest). Table 5.1 shows the mean scores and standard deviations of the assigned rankings for each objective. The table sets out the objectives in order of the importance given to them by:

(a) the total sample of teachers;
(b) the women teachers;
(c) the men teachers.

Table 5.1 Teaching objectives of PE: rankings for total sample, women teachers and men teachers

Rank	Total sample (*n* = 888)	Women (*n* = 433)	Men (*n* = 455)
1	Motor skills *Mean* 3·573, *SD* 2·391	Motor skills *Mean* 3·493, *SD* 2·411	Leisure *Mean* 3·490, *SD* 2·290
2	Self-realisation *Mean* 3·794, *SD* 2·414	Self-realisation *Mean* 3·907, *SD* 2·413	Motor skills *Mean* 3·649, *SD* 2·373
3	Leisure *Mean* 3·855, *SD* 2·369	Emotional stability *Mean* 3·972, *SD* 2·272	Self-realisation *Mean* 3·686, *SD* 2·296
4	Emotional stability *Mean* 4·383, *SD* 2·322	Leisure *Mean* 4·240, *SD* 2·393	Organic developmt *Mean* 4·601, *SD* 2·669
5	Moral developmt *Mean* 4·709, *SD* 2·370	Moral developmt *Mean* 4·809, *SD* 2·354	Moral developmt *Mean* 4·613, *SD* 2·385
6	Social competence *Mean* 5·442, *SD* 2·002	Social competence *Mean* 5·514, *SD* 2·213	Emotional stability *Mean* 4·773, *SD* 2·305
7	Organic developmt *Mean* 5·452, *SD* 2·736	Cognitive developmt *Mean* 5·688, *SD* 2·284	Social competence *Mean* 5·373, *SD* 2·188
8	Cognitive developmt *Mean* 6·084, *SD* 2·275	Organic developmt *Mean* 6·347, *SD* 2·513	Cognitive developmt *Mean* 6·459, *SD* 2·204
9	Aesthetic apprecn *Mean* 6·896, *SD* 2·175	Aesthetic apprecn *Mean* 6·587, *SD* 2·202	Aesthetic apprecn *Mean* 7·188, *SD* 2·110

The objectives given greatest importance by the total sample are motor skills, self-realisation and leisure, while the objectives given the lowest positions are social competence, cognitive development and aesthetic appreciation.

When the mean rankings of the objectives supplied by women teachers are compared with those for the men teachers, a number of interesting results are evident. While motor skills is given very high importance by both men and women, women teachers accorded it the highest rank of the nine objectives listed. Leisure (physical education as a preparation for the enjoyment of leisure time) is ranked highest by men but only fourth among women. Organic development is given a medium rank (fourth) by men but given a relatively low rank (eighth) by women. Emotional stability occupies a position of considerably higher importance among women than among men. Men and women teachers are in reasonable agreement about the relative importance of moral development and aesthetic appreciation. To the former is given the fifth or middle rank of the nine, and to the latter the ninth or lowest position. It might have been expected that moral development would be more highly rated by all, and that aesthetic development would occupy a higher rank among women teachers, since it is commonly believed that as a group they emphasise the art of movement in the physical education curriculum to a greater extent than their men colleagues.

It should be noted in considering the relative importance given to these objectives that apparently *all* the objectives listed are important to physical education teachers according to the literature on the subject. It has already been pointed out that the choice of these nine objectives was made because they were most often mentioned in the wide range of appropriate articles and texts which were reviewed. Respondents' comments indicated that difficulty was experienced by some in ranking these nine objectives, since all the objectives were seen as equally important in an overall view of a balanced physical education programme. A surprisingly large number of teachers accepted the invitation to add their comments on this question. Apart from comments referring to the difficulty of ranking the objectives listed, the teachers offered sixty-one suggestions regarding other objectives which might have been included in some form or other! The most often mentioned additional objectives were concerned with enjoyment and satisfaction in physical education.

OBJECTIVES ACCORDING TO AGE

It might be reasonable to consider that the objectives which teachers emphasise are related to their age. With this in mind, mean scores were assembled on each of the objectives for the five age categories (see Q.4, p. 75) of teachers in the sample. The details are summarised in Table 5.2. The objectives are set down in this table as they were ranked by the total sample of teachers.

There were no large or systematic differences between the mean scores for the five age groups on motor skills, although it may be seen that the youngest teachers rate this objective highest. Similarly, for self-realisation and aesthetic appreciation no real differences between the age groups are evident. On leisure no general trend is discernible, though a substantial difference between the two oldest groups is shown. The biggest difference on emotional stability is between the youngest and the oldest groups, the latter rating this objective

Table 5.2 Teaching objectives according to age

Rank for total sample	Objective		Age group				
			21–22	23–25	26–30	31–39	40 and over
1	Motor skills	Mean	3·26	3·69	3·57	3·44	3·86
		SD	2·30	2·44	2·48	2·20	2·52
2	Self-realisation	Mean	3·87	3·88	3·65	3·72	3·85
		SD	2·52	2·53	2·33	2·36	2·21
3	Leisure	Mean	4·16	3·77	4·10	3·35	4·23
		SD	2·43	2·35	2·41	2·26	2·35
4	Emotional stability	Mean	4·65	4·34	4·31	4·61	3·88
		SD	2·33	2·34	2·36	2·20	2·36
5	Moral developmt	Mean	5·12	4·43	4·87	4·94	4·23
		SD	2·25	2·32	2·45	2·26	2·55
6	Social competence	Mean	5·12	5·19	5·70	5·62	5·74
		SD	2·27	2·24	2·07	2·19	2·18
7	Organic developmt	Mean	5·73	6·03	5·21	4·98	4·76
		SD	2·74	2·66	2·69	2·73	2·72
8	Cognitive developmt	Mean	5·35	6·03	6·16	6·33	6·50
		SD	2·24	2·21	2·26	2·34	2·23
9	Aesthetic apprecn	Mean	6·96	6·83	6·84	6·98	6·95
		SD	2·29	2·23	2·17	2·10	2·07

much higher. The youngest teachers give a much lower rating to moral development and a much higher rating to social competence and cognitive development. Teachers in the two youngest groups also rated organic development lower than their elders. In general, therefore, age appears to be associated with teachers' ranking of objectives. In particular, the youngest group of teachers rank emotional stability, moral development and organic development lower than teachers over twenty-five, but they rank cognitive development and social competence substantially higher.

Facilities

The facilities available may affect, or may be thought to affect, the pursuit of objectives. Heads of departments (*n* = 673) were asked (see Part II, Q.6, pp. 71–2) to judge the adequacy of the facilities they had for their physical education programme. A scale of five categories ranging from 'None or very poor' to 'very good' was used. Table 5.3 gives the percentage of ratings in each category for a number of on-site facilities.

Table 5.3   Adequacy of on-site facilities: percentage of departments in each category ($n = 673$)

Facilities	None or v. poor	Poor	Satis-factory	Good	V. good
Athletics	20	13	34	24	9
Dance	36	12	30	17	5
Gymnastics	7	16	30	32	15
Outdoor games	9	17	27	29	18
Indoor games	18	34	25	13	10
Swimming	65	7	11	8	9
Changing rooms	18	19	32	18	13
Showers	18	16	31	19	16

Facilities for gymnastics and outdoor games were rated by approximately three-quarters of the departmental heads as satisfactory or better; about one-quarter considered that on-site swimming facilities fell into this category. Athletics facilities and both changing and showering accommodation at the school site were regarded as at least satisfactory by two-thirds of the respondents, but suitable spaces for dance and indoor games were considered to be unsatisfactory in about half the departments. Departments may be given a total score for facilities if the five categories of response are assigned scores from 1 (none or very poor) to 5 (very good). As there are eight facilities listed, the maximum range of scores would be from 1 to 40. The mean score for the 673 departments was found to be 21·90, which may be interpreted as indicating that heads of department on average regarded their facilities as being at about the mid-point of the scale, or just satisfactory.

OFF-SITE FACILITIES

Approximately 78% of the heads of departments used off-site facilities for part of their programme. The percentage distribution of these facilities in terms of their perceived adequacy is shown in Table 5.4 for the 521 school departments that used them.

As expected, only a very small percentage of school departments used off-site facilities for dance and gymnastics, but almost two-thirds of them use off-site swimming pools, not all of which were regarded as being up to a satisfactory standard. Rather surprisingly only one-third of the departments using off-site accommodation made use of outdoor games facilities and of

Table 5.4   Adequacy of off-site facilities: percentage of departments
in each category (n = 521)

Facilities	None or not used	Poor	Satis-factory	Good	V. good
Athletics	76	6	7	6	5
Dance	98	1	0	1	0
Gymnastics	99	0	1	0	0
Outdoor games	67	11	11	8	3
Swimming	36	9	23	17	15
Outdoor activity centre	81	1	5	7	6

these almost a third described the facilities as poor. About one in four of these departments used off-site athletics facilities, one-quarter of which were also described as poor.

Travelling time
Since so many schools in the sample used some off-site facilities, it was assumed that some of the time allocated for physical education would necessarily be spent in travelling. Heads of departments were asked to estimate the percentage of physical education time spent on travelling to off-site facilities (see Part II, Q.9, p. 73). Table 5.5 shows the distribution.

Table 5.5   Percentage of PE time spent in travelling:
by proportion of PE departments (n = 673)

% of PE depts	% of time spent in travelling
31	None
22	0– 5
7	6–10
8	11–15
8	16–20
8	21–25
6	26–30
10	Over 30

   Almost a third of the departments were not involved in travelling. Of those who had to travel, 90% estimated that up to 30% of physical education time was spent in journeying to and from the site. About one in three schools apparently use up more than 15% of physical education time travelling, and about one in four use more than 20% in this way.

Changing and showering

Some of physical education time must also be set aside for changing clothes and showering. The departmental heads were therefore asked to estimate how much of the overall time went on these necessary commitments (see Part II, Qs 7–8, pp. 72–3). Tables 5.6 and 5.7 summarise their estimates.

Table 5.6 Percentage of PE time spent in changing: by proportion of PE departments (*n* = 671)

% of PE depts	% of time spent in changing
7	0–5
16	6–10
22	11–15
25	16–20
20	21–25
9	26–30
1	Over 30

More than half the heads of department estimated that more than 15% of the physical education time went on changing and nearly a third put the estimate at over 20%.

With regard to showering the question asked was: 'Estimate the percentage of the overall physical education time spent on showering for the indoor (single period) lesson . . .'

Table 5.7 Percentage of PE time spent in showering: by proportion of PE departments (*n* = 650)

% of PE depts	% of time spent in showering
25	No time
35	0–5
33	6–10
7	11–15

As one-quarter of the respondents indicated that no time was spent on showering, it may be inferred that not only were some schools without showers but also, perhaps, that showering is not regarded as part of the indoor single lesson (see percentage of schools without showers, Table 5.3, p. 38). For the remaining three-quarters, up to 15% of physical education time was estimated for showering, the average time being about 6%.

These estimates for changing and showering may mean that on average it is estimated that more than 20% of physical education time is devoted to these ancillary functions. If travelling is also involved, a much bigger proportion of the allocated time will clearly be required—possibly as much as 30%.

Programme activities

With a view to building up some notion of the content of the physical education programme, a list of activities was assembled from the relevant literature Initially the list consisted of eighty different activities, but these were reduced to a manageable thirty-five (of which five were boys' activities, three girls' activities, and twenty-seven were common to both), on the basis that these were the activities most regularly found in current programmes (see Part II, Q.3, pp. 68–9). This approach towards describing the content of physical education was taken with many misgivings, since many teachers in this field would argue that it might appear to be equating physical education with a list of activities, which would be to misunderstand the meaning and purpose of this aspect of education. Nevertheless, it is true that the activities are the essential constituents of the normal programme through which the teacher attempts to achieve his objectives.

The respondents were asked to indicate which of the listed activities were included in their programmes for each of the secondary years. The number of activities included for each year in each of the 673 departments was recorded, and means and standard deviations computed. Table 5.8 gives the findings.

Table 5.8 Number of PE activities in departmental programmes ($n = 673$ depts)

Year	Mean	SD
1	8·9346	2·2130
2	9·1664	2·3596
3	9·9347	2·7312
4	10·8589	3·1948
5	10·2684	3·7932
6	10·7453	3·8037
7	11·1826	3·5625

The picture presented by Table 5.8 is of a gradual increase in the number of activities from the first to the fourth year, with an associated gradual increase (as shown in the standard deviations) in the spread of the number of

activities offered. The fifth year shows a slight decrease from the fourth year in activities and an increased variation in the number of activities. It has already been shown that the average class time for the schools involved in this enquiry showed a marked decrease in the fifth year. A more obvious decrease in the number of fifth year activities might therefore have been expected. It is likely, however, that in spite of decreased time, the average number of activities remains relatively high in the fifth year (and later) as a result of the introduction at about this time in the secondary school programme of many more options. A more detailed discussion of optional activities is developed later in this chapter.

A further analysis of the number of activities in the programme of boys' and girls' departments seemed to be worthwhile. Table 5.9 gives the interesting comparative statistics which are also represented in histogram form in Fig. 3. While the trend over the years for boys' and girls' departments are similar, reflecting a pattern for the combined sample, there are a number of major differences. The girls have slightly fewer activities in the first year and the difference is increased over the secondary school years. The average number of activities in girls' programmes is therefore seen as increasing very little, whereas the increase for boys is considerable. It may be that in general girls' programmes offer fewer options and concentrate on a smaller number of carefully selected activities. Both the fifth year means show the characteristic decrease, but whereas the boys' means increase for the sixth form years the girls' means do not subsequently recover to the level shown for the fourth year.

Table 5.9 Number of PE activities for boys and girls: by year

Year	Boys' mean	Girls' mean
1	9·241	8·623
2	9·640	8·682
3	10·778	9·068
4	11·910	9·785
5	11·382	9·064
6	12·117	9·321
7	12·521	9·748

ACTIVITY EMPHASIS

Knowing about the number of activities constituting the yearly programmes tells us nothing about the relative amount of time or emphasis given to each

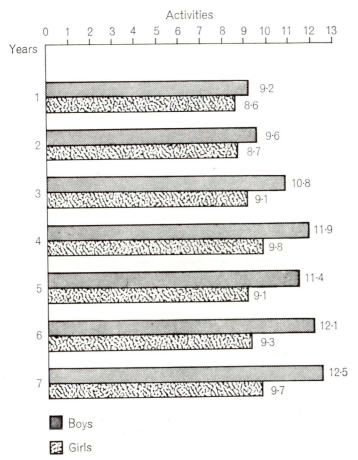

Fig. 3 Comparison of mean scores on PE activities for boys and girls: by year

activity. With a view to getting some idea of the relative emphasis within programmes, the following six groups of activities were identified:

gymnastics;
swimming;
athletics;
dance;
outdoor pursuits;
team games.

Heads of departments ($n = 673$ departments) were asked (Part II, Q.4, p. 69) to indicate the importance they attached to each group of activities in terms of the time given in the physical education programme for each year. The activities were ranked on a scale from 1 (high) to 6 (low), and their means and standard deviations calculated for the first five years of secondary school. The data are given in Tables 5.10–14, which also show the separate rankings for boys' and girls' departments.

Table 5.10   Activity emphasis: year 1

	Total sample			Boys	Girls
Rank	Activity	Mean	SD		
1	Team games	1·5197	0·9662	Team games	Team games
2	Gymnastics	2·1415	1·1275	Gymnastics	Gymnastics
3	Swimming	3·1241	1·2505	Athletics	Swimming
4	Athletics	3·2147	1·0549	Swimming	Athletics
5	Dance	3·8672	1·5184	O/d pursuits	Dance
6	O/d pursuits	4·8605	1·2207	Dance	O/d pursuits

Table 5.11   Activity emphasis: year 2

	Total sample			Boys	Girls
Rank	Activity	Mean	SD		
1	Team games	1·3941	0·7692	Team games	Team games
2	Gymnastics	2·1516	1·0979	Gymnastics	Gymnastics
3	Athletics	3·0744	0·9956	Athletics	Athletics
4	Swimming	3·2762	1·2303	Swimming	Swimming
5	Dance	3·8006	1·4658	O/d pursuits	Dance
6	O/d pursuits	4·7240	1·1996	Dance	O/d pursuits

Table 5.12   Activity emphasis: year 3

	Total sample			Boys	Girls
Rank	Activity	Mean	SD		
1	Team games	1·2917	0·7333	Team games	Team games
2	Gymnastics	2·3732	1·0907	Gymnastics	Gymnastics
3	Athletics	2·8239	0·9819	Athletics	Athletics
4	Swimming	3·3950	1·2279	Swimming	Swimming
5	Dance	3·8924	1·5206	O/d pursuits	Dance
6	O/d pursuits	4·3408	1·3190	Dance	O/d pursuits

Table 5.13   Activity emphasis: year 4

Rank	Activity	Mean	SD	Boys	Girls
	Total sample			Boys	Girls
1	Team games	1·2461	0·7443	Team games	Team games
2	Athletics	2·6981	0·9566	Athletics	Gymnastics
3	Gymnastics	2·7847	1·1677	Gymnastics	Athletics
4	Swimming	3·3718	1·3076	Swimming	Dance
5	Dance	3·8229	1·5904	O/d pursuits	Swimming
6	O/d pursuits	3·9086	1·4738	Dance	O/d pursuits

Table 5.14   Activity emphasis: year 5

Rank	Activity	Mean	SD	Boys	Girls
	Total sample			Boys	Girls
1	Team games	1·2581	0·7707	Team games	Team games
2	Athletics	2·6686	0·9351	Athletics	Gymnastics
3	Gymnastics	3·0080	1·2774	Swimming	Athletics
4	Swimming	3·1885	1·3130	Gymnastics	Dance
5	O/d pursuits	3·5128	1·5632	O/d pursuits	Swimming
6	Dance	3·7032	1·6531	Dance	O/d pursuits

The information given in Tables 5.10–14 indicates that very little change in emphasis occurs over the five years. Team games are clearly in the first ranked position throughout, for the sample as a whole and for both the sub-samples of boys' and girls' departments. Gymnastics and athletics occupy either second or third positions for the five years and swimming occupies fourth position for the first four years. When the ranked positions of these three activity groups are compared for boys' and girls' departments, some differences may be noted (see Appendix D, p. 110). Gymnastics and athletics are seen to feature right through the years of girls' programmes in second and third positions, but swimming for girls drops steadily from third to fifth position. Dance for girls is not highly emphasised (in terms of time devoted to it) at any time but improves from fifth to fourth rank after the third year. Outdoor pursuits holds the lowest position throughout for girls.

The main points worth noting in the ranking of activity groups for boys are that gymnastics, athletics and swimming occupy (in different order) second, third and fourth positions throughout. During the five years gymnastics moves down from second to fourth position, while athletics and swimming both move up one rank. Outdoor pursuits and dance are in fifth and sixth position throughout.

The small amount of change in emphasis in activities for boys' and girls' departments may be appreciated from Figs 4 and 5.

Rank	Activity	Year				
		1	2	3	4	5
1	Team games					
2	Gymnastics					
3	Athletics					
4	Swimming					
5	O/D pursuits					
6	Dance					

Fig. 4 Activity emphasis: boys

Rank	Activity	Year				
		1	2	3	4	5
1	Team games					
2	Gymnastics					
3	Swimming					
4	Athletics					
5	Dance					
6	O/D pursuits					

Fig. 5 Activity emphasis: girls

Teaching styles and approaches to gymnastics

TEACHING STYLES

The way in which the teacher makes use of the curriculum content is an important factor in the planning of learning experiences or in the pursuit of objectives. Methods and styles of teaching may vary according to the demands of different parts of the programme or according to the intended outcomes. All the teachers in the sample ($n = 888$) were asked to estimate how often they used teaching styles described as *direct, guided discovery, problem-*

solving, creative and *individualised programmes* (see Part III, Q.16, p. 77–8). They were asked to consider the programme they taught as a whole and to rate their use of each style on a five-point scale from 1 (never) to 5 (great deal). The means and standard deviations of the estimates were calculated for the total group of teachers and for the men and women separately. Tables 5.15–17 show the rankings and mean scores.

Table 5.15   Teaching styles: total sample (*n* = 888)

Rank	Teaching styles	Mean	SD
1	Guided discovery	3·9367	0·8242
2	Direct	3·6580	0·8710
3	Problem-solving	3·4961	0·8471
4	Creative	2·5366	0·9958
5	Individualised programmes	2·3596	0·9968

Table 5.16   Teaching styles: men (*n* = 455)

Rank	Teaching styles	Mean	SD
1	Direct	3·890	0·804
2	Guided discovery	3·717	0·823
3	Problem-solving	3·288	0·833
4	Individualised programmes	2·421	0·997
5	Creative	2·324	0·953

Table 5.17   Teaching styles: women (*n* = 433)

Rank	Teaching style	Mean	SD
1	Guided discovery	4·166	0·761
2	Problem-solving	3·715	0·806
3	Direct	3·414	0·873
4	Creative	2·760	0·992
5	Individualised programmes	2·296	0·993

In general it is noticeable that both the range of the mean scores and the standard deviations are small. Apparently the teachers did not often estimate at the extreme ends of the scale, i.e. 'never' or 'great deal'. On average, even the lowest ranked style was rated slightly better than 'seldom', while the highest ranked style averaged 'often'.

The styles described as creative and individualised programmes are ranked lowest in all three tables, with mean scores that separate them from the other three styles, which in different order occupy the three highest positions in the three analyses. The combined mean scores for these three most highly emphasised styles of teaching (see Table 5.15) conceal interesting differences between men and women. Table 5.17 shows that women teachers on average give most emphasis to the guided discovery style, for which they record the highest mean score, equivalent to an estimate of better than 'often'. Women rate the problem-solving style somewhat less highly, and direct teaching is rated third, with a mean score that suggests it is used on average somewhat less than 'often'.

In contrast, the men place most emphasis on the direct teaching style. Guided discovery and problem-solving, which are moderately well emphasised, occupy the second and third positions. It might seem that the difference between the men and women may be stated in terms of the women being less committed to styles of teaching which require them to predetermine and directly control the learning sequence, and being more committed to styles which involve the pupil in seeking solutions.

A further investigation of the teachers' rating of styles was undertaken in order to see if there was any correlation between the most often used styles and the age of the teacher. Mean scores on guided discovery, direct teaching and problem-solving were calculated for each of the five age groups and set down in rank order. (For details of this analysis, see Appendix B, pp. 87–9.) The conclusion was that age was related to the emphasis placed by teachers on these three styles. Younger teachers were found to emphasise guided discovery and problem-solving significantly more, and direct teaching significantly less, than older teachers.

APPROACHES TO GYMNASTICS

Gymnastics in some form or other is considered to occupy a position of central importance in most school programmes of physical education. Approximately 94% of the teachers in this sample taught gymnastics. They were asked to estimate the extent to which they made use of five basic approaches: *learning 'principles', movement 'principles', principles of mechanics, physiological 'principles'* and *lead-up stages* (see Part III, Q.17, pp. 78–9). These approaches are not, of course, mutually exclusive. The intention was to get information about the relative use being made of various principles in the teaching of gymnastics. It was thought that this might be helpful in explaining the incidence of the different forms of gymnastics to be found in secondary schools, and might also be useful in explaining objectives held by the teachers. Tables 5.18–20 give the descriptive statistics for the ratings of the total sample, men and women. Ratings were made on a five-point scale from 1 (never) to 5 (great deal).

Table 5.18   Approaches to gymnastics: total sample ($n = 838$)

Rank	Teaching style	Mean	SD
1	Lead-up stages	4·0657	0·9581
2	Movement 'principles'	3·9462	1·0111
3	Learning 'principles'	3·5938	0·9568
4	Principles of mechanics	2·8669	0·9478
5	Physiological 'principles'	2·4431	0·9772

Table 5.19   Approaches to gymnastics: men ($n = 422$)

Rank	Teaching style	Mean	SD
1	Lead-up stages	4·173	0·893
2	Learning 'principles'	3·540	0·960
3	Movement 'principles'	3·528	1·060
4	Principles of mechanics	2·885	0·964
5	Physiological 'principles'	2·720	0·957

Table 5.20   Approaches to gymnastics: women ($n = 416$)

Rank	Teaching style	Mean	SD
1	Movement 'principles'	4·371	0·750
2	Lead-up stages	3·957	1·010
3	Learning 'principles'	3·648	0·951
4	Principles of mechanics	2·848	0·932
5	Physiological 'principles'	2·159	0·915

The lead-up stages approach is highly rated and on average used often by both men and women in their teaching. Movement 'principles' are also often used by the average teacher, and rated very highly by women teachers in particular. Both men and women have a moderately high commitment to learning 'principles' in their teaching of gymnastics, but women apparently seldom base their teaching on physiological 'principles'. The other mean scores indicate that a moderate amount of attention is given by men to physiological 'principles', and by men and women to principles of mechanics. The relatively large standard deviation for movement 'principles' among the men and for the lead-up stages among women shows that there is less agreement, and therefore a greater spread of scores for these two approaches.

When the mean scores on the three highest ranked gymnastics approaches were analysed according to the teachers' age groups, some links were found between the age of the teachers and the use they made of these 'principles'. Older teachers (over thirty) used a movement approach considerably less often than younger teachers, and there was also some evidence for believing that they used learning 'principles' less often. No systematic link between the age of the teachers and the extent of their use of lead-up stages in teaching gymnastics was revealed. (The full details of this analysis are given in Appendix B, pp. 90–1.)

Departmental policy

Another factor which may affect planned outcomes is the departmental teaching policy. In some large schools the policy is to have each member of the physical education department teach his specialism only (e.g. dance, games, swimming, gymnastics), so that a team of experts is available to offer many areas of work to a very high level. In other schools, especially smaller schools, the policy is for the staff to teach over a fairly wide area of the physical education programme (i.e. general teaching of physical education). A third possibility is for a policy which, while requiring the teacher to fulfil commitments in a number of areas, allows him some opportunity for emphasising his specialism. Of course, schools in which there is only one full-time physical education teacher (56% of those in this sample) will have little or no choice of policy regarding staff deployment unless the part-time assistance of other teachers and coaches is available.

The heads of departments were asked to indicate their commitment to *specialist teaching*, *general teaching*, or *general with some emphasis on specialism* (see Part II, Q.10, pp. 73–4). Of the 673 departments involved in the sample, 668 made returns. The percentage response for each of the three types of policy is shown in Table 5.21.

Table 5.21   Extent of specialist/general PE teaching: by departments ($n = 668$)

% of PE depts	Policy
4	Specialist teaching
48	General teaching
48	General with some emphasis on specialism

Only a very small percentage of schools, presumably large ones, organise the teaching of the physical education programme with a team of specialists who teach only their specialism. For the vast majority the choice seems to be for a policy of general teaching or general with some emphasis on specialism, both of which have the same amount of support.

Information was also sought concerning the department's policy about joining with other departments or teachers for integrated (inter-disciplinary) studies. The question put was simply: 'To what extent is your physical education department involved in inter-disciplinary studies within the school ?' Table 5.22 gives the percentage of responses given in each of three categories: 'a great deal', 'a little', and 'not at all'.

Table 5.22 Involvement in inter-disciplinary studies: by departments ($n = 639$)

% of PE depts	Involvement
13	A great deal
48	A little
39	Not at all

Almost two-thirds of the departments are engaged in inter-disciplinary projects to some extent or other. A small percentage (13%) are involved in 'a great deal' of this kind of work and nearly half do 'a little'. This involvement in a collaborative approach to teaching is more widespread than might have been expected and present a picture of a large contribution of physical education resources to the general curriculum of secondary schools.

Degree of compulsion

It was not intended that this enquiry should attempt to find out directly what the pupils felt they needed from the course in physical education, nor whether their particular interests were being satisfied. Increasingly the school programme in physical education has been adapted to satisfy pupils' interests and to cater for differences in needs and abilities. This has been done in many schools by offering pupils, usually in the later years of secondary schooling, some choice of activity during the physical education lesson. Moreover, while attendance at physical education lessons during the first five years of the secondary school is still normally required of all pupils, there is an increasing tendency to have no such compulsion during the sixth form years.

In an effort to discover some details regarding this apparently increasing tendency to offer pupils some choice of activity and to reduce the compulsion for them to attend physical education lessons, a complicated question was structured (see Part II, Q.5, pp. 70–1) and put to heads of departments. Three types of activities were identified in this question:

   (a) *compulsory activities* (CA): pupils must take part and a choice is not given;

(b) *compulsory activities with choice* (CA + C): pupils must take part but a choice is given;

(c) *optional activities* (OA): pupils can opt for one or more activities or opt out of physical education altogether.

The programme (a) to (c) is one of decreasing compulsion and of increasing choice.

The respondents were asked to indicate on a prepared scale the percentage of time given to the three types of activity—CA, CA+C, OA—for each year. Table 5.23 summarises the findings. In each row the difference between the raw total and 100% of respondents is accounted for by non-returns, for which no separate entry is given.

Table 5.23   Compulsory/optional activities: years 1–5

		% of depts by % of time allocated					
Year	Activity type	0%	1–25%	25–50%	51–75%	76–99%	100%
1	CA	0·5	1·8	1·6	4·5	22·5	63·9
	CA+C	64·2	24·1	3·1	0·9	1·5	0·3
	OA	93·5	0·9	0·2	0·0	0·3	0·0
2	CA	1·0	2·5	3·3	6·2	29·0	53·8
	CA+C	54·2	30·3	6·7	1·0	2·2	0·6
	OA	93·9	1·0	0·2	0·0	0·3	0·3
3	CA	2·5	5·5	10·7	14·9	32·1	31·5
	CA+C	32·4	34·5	20·1	4·2	3·9	2·1
	OA	92·6	3·7	0·3	0·0	0·3	0·0
4	CA	15·3	14·9	18·3	18·6	16·6	14·0
	CA+C	18·3	21·3	26·0	11·3	10·3	10·4
	OA	82·6	8·6	3·0	1·2	0·7	1·5
5	CA	35·7	15·9	12·2	11·4	5·9	5·0
	CA+C	17·2	10·4	17·5	10·9	9·8	20·2
	OA	60·6	7·0	4·0	2·8	2·2	9·4

A fairly clear pattern may be seen from Table 5.23 with respect to the decreasing amount of time given to CA over the five years. Nearly two-thirds of the departments (63·9%) have a completely compulsory system operating in the first year, 14% in the fourth year, and only 5% (of a slightly smaller return) in the fifth year. Linked with this huge decrease in the compulsory nature of the programme are increases in choice. The CA+C index shows that in the first year 64·2% of departments have no choice of activity built into

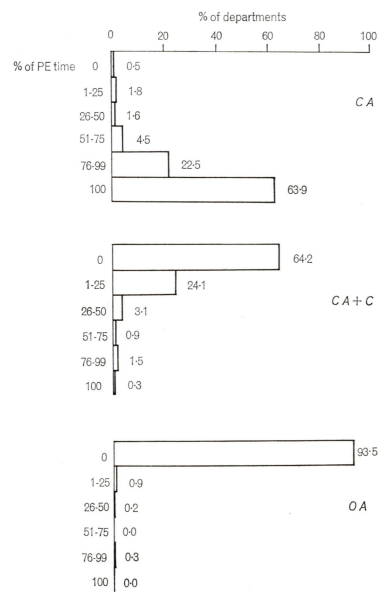

Fig. 6 Degree of compulsion in PE activities: year 1

the programme, but by the fifth year only 17·2% are in this position, and 20% have gone over completely to a CA+C system. The change towards OA, if these data are taken as a trend, is more gradual. The first-year returns show that only about 1% of schools have any OA scheme working and even

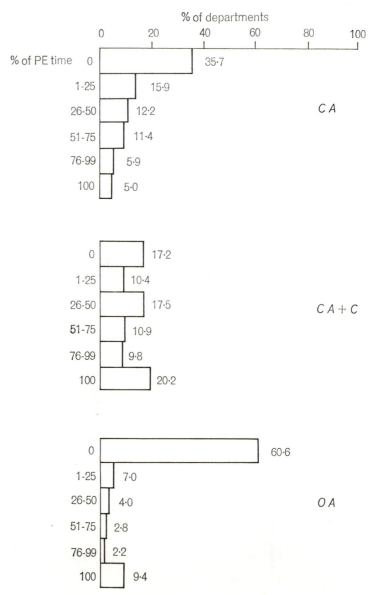

Fig. 7 Degree of compulsion in PE activities: year 5

then for only a small percentage of the physical education time. Thé fourth-year figures record that 15% of schools have some form of an OA scheme in operation and, of the schools with a fifth year, about 10% are fully committed to an OA system, and only 60% or so are without any form of this system.

By way of illustration the details given in Table 5.23 for years 1 and 5 are presented in simplified histogram form in Figures 6 and 7.

The sixth form findings set down in Table 5.24 are for 321 returns for the sixth year and 252 returns for the seventh year.

Table 5.24 Compulsory/optional activities: years 6–7
($n = 321$ and 252 respectively)

Year	Activity type	% of depts by % of time allocated					
		0%	1–25%	26–50%	51–75%	86–99%	100%
6	CA	71·0	11·0	9·0	5·0	3·0	1·0
	CA+C	28·0	7·0	17·0	9·0	8·0	31·0
	OA	52·0	9·0	7·0	4·0	4·0	24·0
7	CA	73·0	9·0	8·0	4·0	3·0	3·0
	CA+C	31·0	9·0	16·0	9·0	6·0	28·0
	OA	48·0	7·0	9·0	3·0	6·0	27·0

Only 1% of departments have completely compulsory (CA) programmes in the sixth year and 71% have no CA at all. This picture is reflected in the findings for CA+C and OA, where 72% have some form of choice (CA+C) and 24% have completely optional schemes (OA). In general the trend towards more choice and less compulsion is seen in the findings for the seventh year.

Pupil effects

Question 22 in Part III of the questionnaire (see pp. 80–2) asked teachers to consider the effects on the pupils of the physical education programme. In a sense this was an enquiry into teachers' perceptions of the outcomes and values of physical education. The question was put in a general form, '. . . you are asked to indicate, in your judgement, the extent to which involvement [of the pupils] in physical education activities contributes to . . . [the listed effects]'. Thirty possible effects of the physical education programme were listed and the teachers were asked to rate each on a five-point scale from 1 ('great deal') to 5 ('little or none'). A 'not sure' response was coded as zero and excluded from the subsequent calculations. Three statistics were computed for each of the thirty items—the mean score, the standard deviation, and the response n. The value of n was the maximum ($n = 850$), minus the zero values for the item, and may be regarded as an index of uncertainty. Table 5.25 gives these descriptive statistics and the rank order of each item according to the mean value.

Table 5.25   Teachers' views of the extent to which involvement in PE activities contributes to pupil effects (*n* = 852 overall)

Effect	Great deal	Moderately		Little or none	Not sure	Mean	SD	n	Rank
	1	2	3	4	5 0				
(1) Positive attitude to school	1	2	3	4	5 0	2·3	1·1	827	12=
(2) Muscular strength and endurance	1	2	3	4	5 0	2·5	1·1	843	16=
(3) Ability to persist in difficulties	1	2	3	4	5 0	3·0	1·1	838	25=
(4) Awareness of movement themes	1	2	3	4	5 0	3·0	1·2	826	25=
(5) Independent thinking	1	2	3	4	5 0	2·7	1·1	845	21
(6) Remedy physical defects	1	2	3	4	5 0	3·7	1·2	820	30
(7) Effective relationships	1	2	3	4	5 0	2·5	1·1	826	16=
(8) Motivation to achieve in areas other than PE	1	2	3	4	5 0	3·4	1·2	811	29
(9) Wide-ranging interests inside and outside school	1	2	3	4	5 0	2·5	1·2	836	16=
(10) Cardio-vascular endurance	1	2	3	4	5 0	2·8	1·2	819	22=
(11) Ability to communicate through movement	1	2	3	4	5 0	3·2	1·3	806	28
(12) Self-confidence outside the PE situation	1	2	3	4	5 0	2·2	0·9	839	9=
(13) Thinking before taking action	1	2	3	4	5 0	2·9	1·2	814	24
(14) Motor co-ordination	1	2	3	4	5 0	2·1	0·9	837	6=
(15) Self-discipline	1	2	3	4	5 0	2·3	1·0	838	12=
(16) Enjoyment of participation in physical activity	1	2	3	4	5 0	1·4	0·7	846	1
(17) Ability to take the initiative in a situation	1	2	3	4	5 0	2·6	0·9	835	19=
(18) Making allowance for others' deficiencies	1	2	3	4	5 0	2·8	1·2	841	22=
(19) Understanding the other's point of view	1	2	3	4	5 0	3·1	1·1	834	27
(20) Positive attitude to authority in general	1	2	3	4	5 0	2·6	1·1	831	19=
(21) Motivation to achieve in PE	1	2	3	4	5 0	2·1	0·9	836	6=
(22) Wide range of movement skills	1	2	3	4	5 0	2·1	1·0	841	6=
(23) Awareness of one's own deficiencies	1	2	3	4	5 0	2·3	1·1	839	12=
(24) General self-confidence	1	2	3	4	5 0	2·0	0·9	841	4=

Table 5.25—*cont.*

Effect	Great deal	Moderately	Little or none	Not sure			Mean	SD	n	Rank
	1	2	3	4	5	0				
(25) Sense of responsibility	1	2	3	4	5	0	2·4	1·0	836	15
(26) Ability to get on with others	1	2	3	4	5	0	2·2	1·0	847	9=
(27) General physical development	1	2	3	4	5	0	2·0	1·0	843	4=
(28) Appreciation of limitations and capabilities	1	2	3	4	5	0	2·2	1·0	840	9=
(29) Satisfaction from success in physical activity	1	2	3	4	5	0	1·5	0·7	846	2
(30) Release from tensions that develop during school day	1	2	3	4	5	0	1·8	1·0	846	3

The highest ranked items are assembled in Table 5.26. The teachers placed the items describing enjoyment and satisfaction in the first two positions, and associated statistics show that they were in strong agreement and felt very certain of their view. This strongly held view that enjoyment and satisfaction are the main effects of participation in physical education activities, while somewhat unexpected, is in accord with a number of the teachers' written comments, which suggest enjoyment and satisfaction as important objectives of physical education. The other highly ranked items refer to release from tension, physical development, self-confidence and acquisition of skills as being the most likely outcomes.

Table 5.26   Highest ranked pupil effects

Rank	Effect	Item
1	Enjoyment of participation in physical activity	16
2	Satisfaction from success in physical activity	29
3	Release from tensions that develop during school day	30
4 =	General self-confidence	24
4 =	General physical development	27
6 =	Motor co-ordination	14
6 =	Motivation to achieve in PE	21
6 =	Wide range of movement skills	22

Table 5.27 Lowest ranked pupil effects

Rank	Effect	Item
25 =	Ability to persist in face of difficulties	3
25 =	Awareness of movement themes	4
27	Understanding the other's point of view	19
28	Ability to communicate through movement	11
29	Motivation to achieve in areas other than PE	8
30	Remedy physical defects	6

Table 5.27 gives the six items with the lowest mean ratings. Rather surprisingly, item 6 (remedy physical defects) has the lowest value (and a high index of disagreement). In the earlier days of physical education in Britain there was certainly a very high commitment to the remedying of minor physical defects, so that this finding may well represent an important measure of change. Other poorly rated items seem to be those with less precise operational definitions and vaguer meanings. This is inferred from their relatively low *n* values and relatively high standard deviations.

With a view to reporting the teachers' views on the effects of physical education in simple terms, the ratings on the items were intercorrelated, and a factor analysis undertaken. The purpose of this was to see how items answered in the same way clustered together. Seven major clusters, or factors, were identified, and these represent the major dimensions underlying the teachers' views on the effects listed. Table 5.28 describes and lists in order of size and importance the seven factors, together with the main items which contribute to them. The details of the analysis are given in Appendix C, pp. 92–4.

The largest factor considered by the teachers to denote the most important effect, is describe as *social awareness and responsibility*. It assumes, perhaps surprisingly, a position of greater importance than *general physical develop-*

Table 5.28 Pupil effects: major factors

Factor	Items
(i) Social awareness and responsibility	18, 19, 26
(ii) General physical development	10, 2, 27
(iii) Self-awareness	23, 28, 29
(iv) General movement ability	4, 22, 5
(v) General interest in school	9, 1, 8
(vi) Enjoyment in physical activity	16, 11
(vii) Cognitive judgement	13, 15, 17

ment, which might have been expected to be in the highest rank. Factors five and seven describe interesting and related groupings of effects which the teachers consider to be likely outcomes. Together these seven factors appear adequately and meaningfully to describe the major dimensions of perceived effects arising from the physical education programme.

In order to investigate possible differences between the views of men and women teachers, and also to consider teachers' views according to their age group, some further analyses were undertaken. These were limited to a comparison by sex and age of the three largest factors. For each teacher a score on these three factors was computed. The means of these scores for men and women and for the five age groups of teachers (see Q.4, p. 75) were assembled and compared. (The comparative analyses are reported in Appendix C, pp. 94–8.) The main findings were that the women scored significantly higher than men on general physical development, and that there was a significant trend with age on this same factor and on social awareness and responsibility. In both cases younger teachers had the higher scores.

These are somewhat unexpected results. While younger teachers might be expected to rate the social effects of physical education more highly than their older colleagues, the latter are usually thought to regard physical development as of major importance. Moreover, men teachers of physical education are generally thought to attach higher prestige to physical development than women. These findings might have been expected to be in accord with the ranking of objectives by men and women teachers, but some unexplained incongruities clearly exist.

6 Concluding remarks

The enquiry which is reported here was intended to be a survey of factual information. In the process of planning and operation, some extensions and adaptations took place. Some probing into teachers' attitudes and perceptions, for instance, was undertaken to give meaning to the basic statistics. Nevertheless, the report is essentially a collection of factual information about the physical education curriculum. It gives some information about all the areas of the curriculum that were mentioned in the brief (see p. 1). There are other aspects that might have been investigated, and certainly some of those covered here require further research in depth. It was regretted, for instance, that no children were interviewed or asked to supply information. Without some knowledge of their attitudes, interests and involvement, one of the main elements which needs to be considered in curriculum planning will be missing.

It is unnecessary to summarise here the main findings. In the body of the report short summaries are given at the openings of chapters. It would also be going beyond the terms of reference to make recommendations arising from the report, though the intention of those who commissioned the enquiry was that the findings should be the descriptive basis on which a curriculum development project would be developed (see p. 1).

Aims and objectives
This report contains general foundations for the development of a curriculum methodology. The first of these might be long-term educational aims and short-term objectives. In this enquiry the nine teaching objectives listed included what some would describe as aims. The fact is that most of the pertinent physical education literature fails to distinguish clearly between aims and objectives, and it was from this literature that the objectives of physical education were identified for the purposes of the enquiry. Nevertheless, the findings from this investigation with regard to objectives may well serve as a cornerstone for curriculum planning. The questionnaire results, together with the evidence supplied on this topic by the teachers, in their written comments and at the interviews, represents a most valuable collection of information concerning the emphasis placed on a wide range of aims and objectives.

Curriculum content

The curriculum content, i.e. what the teachers are to teach, is often what concerns the teacher most, and may be considered the second fundamental area for curriculum planning. The report gives details of the activities that constitute existing school programmes and the relative emphasis placed on them. It outlines the way in which the system of pupil choice of activities works over the years and the way in which the programme of activities is extended through extra-curricular opportunities. Linked closely with the curriculum content are the methods employed in teaching it. The enquiry has produced information about the use of different teaching styles and strategies, and has probed, in particular, the approaches used in the teaching of the centrally important area of gymnastics.

The amount of time available is another related aspect of the teaching context. In Chapter 2 an account is given of the amount of time available throughout the secondary years for physical education. The 'real' time which may be used is, of course, affected by special factors operating in physical education, including time required for changing, showering and travelling. On the credit side, however, is the additional time used outside the curriculum allocation by the vast majority of teachers.

The enquiry also considered a number of factors which might influence the teacher in carrying out his perceived functions, and it was found, for instance, that physical education teachers felt that the total work commitment expected of them, the diversity of students they were required to teach, and the resources available to them limited their effectiveness considerably.

Effectiveness

The ways of assessing the effectiveness of the planned courses form a third major consideration in curriculum planning. Information is given in the report about the pupil effects that teachers consider result from present physical education programmes. This information would indicate that these teachers see a great deal more than physical development coming from their courses, and would justify some of their highly rated objectives. They see the development of self-awareness and interpersonal awareness, and a heightened sense of enjoyment and satisfaction in their pupils, as well as the expected improvement in physical abilities.

There is necessarily no possibility of assessing the contribution, rated very highly by some headmasters, which is indirectly made by physical education to the general education of children. The pupils concerned include some who are not highly gifted or motivated in other directions and for whom the physical education curriculum provides a sphere in which relationships with staff grow to the point at which total education begins. For these pupils, physical education in schools has a particular and perhaps a unique value.

On the basis of the current information supplied by teachers concerning fundamental aspects of curriculum planning and operation, a rewarding and useful curriculum development project could well be planned. The interviews that were held emphasised the teachers' wish for help and guidance in curriculum planning, and the enquiry findings showed up a number of incongruities between the objectives, the teaching styles and the effects of programmes.

What is clear from the enquiry is that physical education teachers deserve whatever assistance they can get. They are dedicated (averaging an additional eight hours of unpaid extra-curricular service each week), have a broad educational commitment, and consider that successful teaching in physical education depends on social concern, wide professional education and an enlightened capacity for sustained hard work.

Appendix A   Questionnaire

This questionnaire has been constructed in order to provide information about the circumstances under which physical education forms part of the secondary school programme in England and Wales.

This information will not only provide a descriptive report of facts and opinions concerning the physical education curriculum, but will also serve as a firm basis for a curriculum development project. Your answers will therefore be of great value.

The questionnaire is confidential. Neither the name of the school nor the identity of respondents will be revealed in any way.

Part I

(To be completed by head or deputy head.)

GENERAL SCHOOL INFORMATION PROFILE

For each question below you will see that boxes or spaces are provided for your response. Write in the answer or tick the box which is appropriate to your school.

1. *Name of school* ....
....

2. *Type of school*
   Grammar, maintained   ☐ *1*
   Grammar, direct grant   ☐ *2*
   Secondary modern   ☐ *3*
   Comprehensive   ☐ *4*

Junior high	☐ *5*
Senior high	☐ *6*
Independent	☐ *7*
Technical	☐ *8*

3. *Current roll*

Less than 299	☐ *1*
300–399	☐ *2*
400–599	☐ *3*
600–799	☐ *4*
800–1000	☐ *5*
Over 1000	☐ *6*

4. *Number of teaching staff*

Full-time	......
Part-time	......

5. *Catchment area*

Mainly urban	☐ *1*
Mainly suburban	☐ *2*
Mainly rural	☐ *3*

6. *Housing description*

Majority of pupils' homes owner occupied	☐ *1*
Approximately half of pupils' homes rented, half owner occupied	☐ *2*
Majority of pupils' homes rented	☐ *3*

7. *Pupils' fathers' occupations*

Majority of pupils' fathers in non-manual occupations	☐ *1*
Approximately half of pupils' fathers in manual, half in non-manual occupations	☐ *2*
Majority of pupils' fathers in manual occupations	☐ *3*

8. *Approximate percentage of immigrant pupils in the school*   ......

9. *School organisation*

Basically streamed	☐ *1*
Basically unstreamed	☐ *2*
Other	☐ *3*

If (3), please describe briefly your situation below:

....

....

10. *General timetable information*
    Timetable cycle of 5 days   ☐ *1*
    6 days   ☐ *2*
    7 days   ☐ *3*
    8 days   ☐ *4*
    9 days   ☐ *5*
    10 days   ☐ *6*
    Other (give details):

    ....

    ....

11. *Average class time*
    For the purpose of arriving at an 'average class time' for certain curri-
    culum subjects the following tables have been assembled. Information is
    required for each year regarding the total number of periods in one
    timetable cycle, the number of forms taking the subject in each year and
    the length of a single period for each of the selected subjects. In many
    schools, forms in the same year have a different number of periods in the
    same subject, therefore in the first column give the total number of
    periods per cycle for all the forms in a year group.

Combined total of periods for all forms within year	No. of forms taking the subject	Length of a single period in minutes	*Please leave this column blank*
Year 1 (*12 year olds*)			
English	....	....	....
Mathematics	....	....	....
Geography	....	....	....
History	....	....	....
Physical education (including games)	....	....	....
Year 2 (*13 year olds*)			
English	....	....	....
Mathematics	....	....	....
Geography	....	....	....
History	....	....	....
Physical education (including games)	....	....	....

	Combined total of periods for all forms within year	No. of forms taking the subject	Length of a single period in minutes	*Please leave this column blank*
Year 3 (14 year olds)				
English	......	......	......	......
Mathematics	......	......	......	......
Geography	......	......	......	......
History	......	......	......	......
Physical education (including games)	......	......	......	......
Year 4 (15 year olds)				
English	......	......	......	......
Mathematics	......	......	......	......
Geography	......	......	......	......
History	......	......	......	......
Physical education (including games)	......	......	......	......
Year 5 (16 year olds)				
English	......	......	......	......
Mathematics	......	......	......	......
Geography	......	......	......	......
History	......	......	......	......
Physical education (including games)	......	......	......	......
Year 6 (17 year olds)				
English	......	......	......	......
Mathematics	......	......	......	......
Geography	......	......	......	......
History	......	......	......	......
Physical education (including games)	......	......	......	......
Year 7 (18 year olds)				
English	......	......	......	......
Mathematics	......	......	......	......
Geography	......	......	......	......
History	......	......	......	......
Physical education (including games)	......	......	......	......

THANK YOU

Part II

To be completed by the head of the physical education department or the teacher responsible for physical education. For the purposes of this questionnaire, in mixed schools the boys' and girls' departments should be considered separately and each head of department is asked to complete this section. (Two copies of Part II are provided for mixed schools.)

When you have completed the questionnaire please secure the opening edge with some form of sealing tape and return to the head teacher for mailing.

For each question, boxes or spaces are provided for your response. Write in the answer or tick the box which is appropriate to your school.

1. *Name of school* ....

....

Information in this section is given by:
Head of boys' physical education   ☐ *1*
Head of girls' physical education   ☐ *2*

2. *Staffing*

Number of teachers appointed to teach physical education full-time   ......

Number of teachers appointed to teach physical education part-time   ......

Number of other members of staff who assist with timetabled physical education   ......

Number of other members of staff who assist with extra-curricular physical education   ......

Number of qualified coaches/instructors (unqualified teachers) who assist with timetabled physical education   ......

Number of qualified coaches/instructors (unqualified teachers) who assist with extra-curricular physical education   ......

3. *Physical education timetable*

Printed on the chart below is a list of activities many of which are found regularly in physical education curriculum programmes. Tick those activities taken during any term in each of the years in your school.

	Year 1	Year 2	Year 3	Year 4	Year 5	Year 6	Year 7
Archery	......	......	......	......	......	......	......
Association football	......	......	......	......	......	......	......
Athletics	......	......	......	......	......	......	......
Badminton	......	......	......	......	......	......	......
Basketball	......	......	......	......	......	......	......
Bowling	......	......	......	......	......	......	......
Boxing	......	......	......	......	......	......	......
Canoeing	......	......	......	......	......	......	......
Cricket	......	......	......	......	......	......	......
Cross-country	......	......	......	......	......	......	......
Dance (modern educational)	......	......	......	......	......	......	......
Dance (folk, other)	......	......	......	......	......	......	......
Fencing	......	......	......	......	......	......	......
Golf	......	......	......	......	......	......	......
Gymnastics (educational)	......	......	......	......	......	......	......
Gymnastics (Olympic)	......	......	......	......	......	......	......
Hockey (boys)	......	......	......	......	......	......	......
Hockey (girls)	......	......	......	......	......	......	......
Judo	......	......	......	......	......	......	......
Keep fit	......	......	......	......	......	......	......
Lacrosse	......	......	......	......	......	......	......
Lawn tennis	......	......	......	......	......	......	......
Netball	......	......	......	......	......	......	......
Orienteering	......	......	......	......	......	......	......
Rounders	......	......	......	......	......	......	......
Rowing	......	......	......	......	......	......	......
Rugby League Football	......	......	......	......	......	......	......
Rugby Union Football	......	......	......	......	......	......	......
Skating (ice)	......	......	......	......	......	......	......
Skating (roller)	......	......	......	......	......	......	......
Swimming	......	......	......	......	......	......	......

	Year 1	Year 2	Year 3	Year 4	Year 5	Year 6	Year 7
Table tennis	......	......	......	......	......	......	......
Trampolining	......	......	......	......	......	......	......
Volleyball	......	......	......	......	......	......	......
Weight training	......	......	......	......	......	......	......
Leave blank	......	......	......	......	......	......	......

4. *Emphasis on various groups of activities in the physical education programme*
Different aspects of the physical education programme are emphasised in
different schools. Below is a list of some major areas of the programme
which you are asked to consider in terms of the emphasis placed upon
them in your school. The list is not inetnded to be exhaustive.

Gymnastics	...	...	...	...	...	...	...	...	A
Swimming	...	...	...	...	...	...	...	...	B
Athletics	...	...	...	...	...	...	...	...	C
Dance ...	...	...	...	...	...	...	...	...	D
Outdoor pursuits	...	...	...	...	...	...	...	E
Team games	...	...	...	...	...	...	...	...	F

On the table below indicate the importance attached to each area, in terms of
the time given in your physical education curriculum programme, by ranking
them for each year. Place (1) against the most important area, (2) against
the next in importance and so on until (6). Where an area is not included in
the year's programme rank it 0. If possible, avoid giving equal rankings but
where two areas are emphasised equally in your timetable give these areas the
same rank and omit the next lowest rank number.
E.g. If team games (F) and swimming (B) are equal second, rank each with the
number (2), omit (3) and continue with (4) for the fourth ranking.

	A	B	C	D	E	F
Year 1 ranks	......	......	......	......	......	......
Year 2 ranks	......	......	......	......	......	......
Year 3 ranks	......	......	......	......	......	......
Year 4 ranks	......	......	......	......	......	......
Year 5 ranks	......	......	......	......	......	......

5. *Degree of compulsion*

It would be useful to have an approximate indication of the extent of compulsion in your physical education programme, and this is described under three headings:

COMPULSORY ACTIVITIES (CA): Pupils must take part and a choice is not given.
Example: A form has three periods of physical education per week; all pupils have gymnastics for the first, all have association football for the second and all have swimming for the third lesson.

COMPULSORY ACTIVITIES WITH CHOICE (CA + C): Pupils must take part but a choice is given.
Example: A form has three periods of physical education per week. Pupils have a choice between dance and gymnastics for the first, between table tennis and badminton for the second, and a choice of hockey or netball or lacrosse for the third lesson. Therefore pupils are engaged in some form of physical activity for the three periods.

OPTIONAL ACTIVITIES (OA): Pupils can opt for one or more activities or opt out of physical education altogether.
Example: Pupils may decide to take up one or more activities offered or spend their time in some other non-physical education pursuit—a hobby, reading, etc.

In the table below please indicate (by ticking the appropriate spaces) the approximate percentage of the time given to physical education which falls into the above three categories CA, CA+C, OA for each year. There should be three ticks for each year.

Example: If in the first year approximately half a term (either as a total of periods or a block of time) is devoted to CA+C, this amounts to roughly one-sixth of the total year time (6 half-terms) or approximately 16%. Hence the space marked 1–25% opposite CA+C would be ticked. A tick in the space marked 76–99% opposite CA would indicate that the rest of the year's programme is compulsory and the third tick would be placed in the box marked 0% opposite OA.

	0%	1–25%	26–50%	51–75%	76–99%	100%
Year 1						
CA	......	......	......	......	✓	......
CA+C	......	✓	......	......	......	......
OA	✓	......	......	......	......	......

	1	2	3	4	5	6
	0%	1–25%	26–50%	51–75%	76–99%	100%

Year 1

CA	......	......	......	......	......	......
CA+C	......	......	......	......	......	......
OA	......	......	......	......	......	......

Year 2

CA	......	......	......	......	......	......
CA+C	......	......	......	......	......	......
OA	......	......	......	......	......	......

Year 3

	......	......	......	......	......	......
CA	......	......	......	......	......	......
CA+C	......	......	......	......	......	......
OA	......	......	......	......	......	......

Year 4

CA	......	......	......	......	......	......
CA+C	......	......	......	......	......	......
OA	......	......	......	......	......	......

Year 5

CA	......	......	......	......	......	......
CA+C	......	......	......	......	......	......
OA	......	......	......	......	......	......

Year 6

CA	......	......	......	......	......	......
CA+C	......	......	......	......	......	......
OA	......	......	......	......	......	......

Year 7

CA	......	......	......	......	......	......
CA+C	......	......	......	......	......	......
OA	......	......	......	......	......	......

6. *Physical education facilities*

You are asked to judge the degree of adequacy of your physical education facilities in relation to your physical education programme by ticking the appropriate column. (If non-existent, tick 'very poor'.)

ON SCHOOL SITE

	1	2	3	4	5	6
Facilities	None	Very poor	Poor	Satis-factory	Good	Very good
Athletics	......	......	......	......	......	......
Dance	......	......	......	......	......	......
Gymnastics	......	......	......	......	......	......
Outdoor games	......	......	......	......	......	......
Indoor games	......	......	......	......	......	......
Swimming	......	......	......	......	......	......
Changing rooms	......	......	......	......	......	......
Showers	......	......	......	......	......	......

Do you use off-site facilities for part of the physical education programme?

    Yes   ☐ 1
    No   ☐ 2

If 'yes' please indicate in the following table the adequacy of these facilities as you did above, if 'no' proceed to the next question.

OFF SCHOOL SITE

	1	2	3	4	5
Facilities	Very poor	Poor	Satis-factory	Good	Very good
Athletics	......	......	......	......	......
Dance	......	......	......	......	......
Gymnastics	......	......	......	......	......
Outdoor games	......	......	......	......	......
Indoor games	......	......	......	......	......
Swimming	......	......	......	......	......
Outdoor activity centre	......	......	......	......	......

7. *Changing*

All physical education programmes involve pupils changing their clothes to a certain extent. Estimate the percentage of the physical education time, 'pre' and 'post' lesson, spent on changing for the 'indoor' (single period) lesson by ticking the appropriate box.

0–5%	☐	1
6–10%	☐	2
11–15%	☐	3
16–20%	☐	4
21–25%	☐	5
26–30%	☐	6
Over 30%	☐	7

8. *Showering*

Estimate the percentage of the overall physical education time spent on showering for the 'indoor' (single period) lesson by ticking the appropriate box.

No time	☐	1
0–5%	☐	2
6–10%	☐	3
11–15%	☐	4

9. *Travelling*

Many physical education programmes necessitate travel to off-site facilities and this invariably means that some physical education time is used for travelling. Estimate the percentage of physical education time spent on travelling (if undertaken) to off-site facilities by ticking the appropriate box.

No travel	☐	0
0–5%	☐	1
6–10%	☐	2
11–15%	☐	3
16–20%	☐	4
21–25%	☐	5
26–30%	☐	6
Over 30%	☐	7

10. *Physical education policy*

In some schools the policy is to have each member of the physical education staff teach his specialism (e.g. specialist in dance, games, swimming). In other schools the policy is for the physical education staff to teach all areas (general teaching) or for the timetable to be arranged so that there is general teaching with some emphasis on specialisms. Please tick the appropriate box.

In this department the policy is towards:

specialist teaching	☐ *1*
general teaching	☐ *2*
general with some emphasis on specialism	☐ *3*

To what extent is your physical education department involved in interdisciplinary studies within the school?

a great deal	☐ *1*
a little	☐ *2*
not at all	☐ *3*

THANK YOU

Part III

To be completed by each full-time member of staff who teaches physical education.

When you have completed the questionnaire please secure the opening edge with some form of sealing tape and return to the head teacher for mailing.

BIOGRAPHICAL INFORMATION

1. *Name of school* ....

2. *Your name* ....
   (Be anonymous if you wish, although your name would be useful for possible follow-up.)

Circle the appropriate number in the following items

3. *Present status*

   Assistant teacher of physical education *1*

   Head or in charge of physical education dept:

boys' school	*2*
girls' school	*3*
boys (in mixed school)	*4*
girls (in mixed school)	*5*
mixed school	*6*

4. *Age*

21–22	*1*
23–25	*2*
26–30	*3*
31–39	*4*
40 and over	*5*

5. *Sex*

Female	*1*
Male	*2*

6. *Marital status*

Single	*1*
Married without children	*2*
Married with child(ren)	*3*

7. *Type of secondary school last attended as pupil*

Comprehensive	*1*
Grammar, direct grant	*2*
Grammar, maintained	*3*
Independent	*4*
Secondary modern	*5*
Technical	*6*
School outside Britain	*7*

8. *GCE A level or equivalent examinations you have passed*

A level	None	*0*
arts or	One subject	*1*
humanities	Two subjects	*2*
	Three subjects	*3*
A level	None	*0*
sciences	One subject	*1*
	Two subjects	*2*
	Three subjects	*3*

Other equivalent examinations (please specify):

....

....

9. *Are you a:*

Non-graduate?	*1*
Graduate?	*2*
If graduate state degree(s)	

10. *How was your specialist teacher qualification in physical education gained?*
Third-year supplementary one-year course *1*
Three-year continuous course *2*
One-year course for graduates *3*
Other (please specify):
....
....

11. *How many years have you been teaching as a specialist physical education teacher in secondary schools?*
Less than 1 year *1*
1–3 years *2*
4–6 years *3*
7–9 years *4*
10–12 years *5*
13–15 years *6*
More than 15 years *7*

12. *At present are you regularly teaching any other subject(s) in your school?*
Yes *1*
No *2*

13. *Before becoming a specialist teacher of physical education were you in full-time employment in any other occupation or profession?*
No *0*
Less than 1 year *1*
1–5 years *2*
6–10 years *3*
More than 10 years *4*

14. *Increasing opportunities are now available for teachers to undertake higher level study. What is the most advanced qualification you aim for?* (Circle one only.)
No plans at present *0*
B.Ed. *1*
B.A./B.Sc. *2*
Advanced Diploma in a specialisation *3*
M.A./M.Phil., etc. *4*
Ph.D. *5*

OBJECTIVES IN THE TEACHING OF PHYSICAL EDUCATION

15. The following objectives of physical education are regularly found in the literature on the subject. You are asked to rank these objectives by

placing (1) against the one you consider to be the most important, (2) against the next important, and so on until (9). If possible, avoid giving equal rankings, but where you consider two objectives to be of equal importance give these the same rank number and omit the next lowest rank number.

Read the entire list and explanations before commencing your rankings.

Emotional stability (refers to the opportunities given for the development of personal control and personal adjustment)   ......

Self-realisation (refers to the opportunities offered to each individual to capitalise on his unique abilities)   ......

Leisure-time activities (refers to the opportunities given for acquiring appropriate physical pursuits for the enjoyment of leisure time)   ......

Social competence (refers to the contribution to the development of interpersonal skills)   ......

Moral development (refers to the contribution to the development of desirable standards of behaviour and conduct)   ......

Organic development (refers to the development of optimum functioning of the cardiovascular and other organic systems)   ......

Motor skills (refers to the development of general co-ordination and efficiency in movement and in the more specific skills required in athletics, dance, games, etc.)   ......

Aesthetic appreciation (refers to the development of an understanding of aesthetic criteria, values and judgements)   ......

Cognitive development (refers to the contribution to the development of reasoning and the making of judgements)   ......

If you feel that in your teaching of physical education you have objectives not specified above, please state these briefly:

....

....

TEACHING STYLES AND APPROACHES

16. Different parts of the physical education programme may call for different teaching styles. Taking the programme you teach as a whole, estimate in the table below how often you use the following styles.

	Never	Seldom	Occa-sionally	Often	Great deal
Direct (the teacher predetermines the objectives and the precise learning sequence)	1	2	3	4	5
Guided discovery (the teacher is constantly setting the appropriate learning situations so that the student himself gains pertinent knowledge or understanding)	1	2	3	4	5
Problem-solving (the teacher poses the problems and the student is expected to seek the solution or solutions)	1	2	3	4	5
Creative (the student selects the problem, examines it and proposes innovative solutions)	1	2	3	4	5
Individualised programmes (the teacher prepares individual programmes geared to the needs of particular students)	1	2	3	4	5

17. *Gymnastics*

Do you teach gymnastics ? Yes 1

No 2

If 'yes' answer the following, if 'no' proceed to question 18.

The teaching of some form of gymnastics is probably included in most physical education programmes. There would seem to be a variety of approaches used. In general, in your teaching of gymnastics, estimate to what extent you make use of each approach.

	Never	Seldom	Occa-sionally	Often	Great deal
Learning 'principles' (e.g. motivation)	1	2	3	4	5
Movement 'principles' (e.g. time, weight, space, flow)	1	2	3	4	5
Principles of mechanics (e.g. action and reaction)	1	2	3	4	5
Physiological 'principles' (e.g. 'overload')	1	2	3	4	5
Lead-up stages (progressive stages in the teaching of a skill)	1	2	3	4	5

EXTRA-CURRICULAR ACTIVITIES

These are defined as those activities outside the normal timetable in which physical education teachers are often involved as part of their work.

18. *Time*

Ring the appropriate numbers in the following table to indicate the times when you are regularly involved in extra-curricular activities.

	Yes	No
Before school	1	0
Lunch-time	1	0
Immediately following afternoon school or evening	1	0
Saturday a.m....	1	0
Sunday p.m.	1	0

19. *Duration*

Estimate the total number of hours in a normal school week in which you are involved in extra-curricular activities

Up to 3 hours	1
3 hours or more but less than 6 hours	2
6 9	3
9 12	4
12 15	5
15 18	6
18 21	7
21 hours or more	8

20. *Activities*

Ring the appropriate numbers in the following table to indicate whether or not you are regularly involved in the teaching of these extra-curricular activities:

							Yes	*No*
Team games ...	...	...	...	...	...		*1*	*0*
Gymnastics ...	...	...	...	...	...		*1*	*0*
Dance	...	...	...	...	...		*1*	*0*
Swimming ...	...	...	...	...	...		*1*	*0*
Athletics ...	...	...	...	...	...		*1*	*0*
Outdoor activities ...	...	...	...	...			*1*	*0*
Other ...	...	...	...	...	...	...	*1*	*0*

21. *Membership*

Some extra-curricular activities are open to all pupils, in others teachers make some form of selection and in a few activities membership depends entirely upon the pupils' ability.

In relation to your own extra-curricular activities circle the appropriate numbers to indicate your method of selecting pupils.

Membership	Activities				
	None	Few	About half	Most	All
Open membership	*1*	*2*	*3*	*4*	*5*
Partially selective membership (e.g. teacher's discretion)	*1*	*2*	*3*	*4*	*5*
Membership through ability	*1*	*2*	*3*	*4*	*5*

PUPIL EFFECTS

The purpose of this section of the questionnaire is to seek your help in ascertaining the significance of certain effects which may result from participation in physical education activities.

22. A list is given below of a number of pupil effects which may result from participation in physical education activities. This is not an exhaustive list and space has been left at the bottom of the column to add any significant items you think have been overlooked.

Opposite each effect you are asked to indicate, in your judgement, the extent to which involvement in physical education activities contributes to the particular effect, by circling the appropriate number.

Pupil effects	A great deal		Mod- erate		Little or none	Not sure
	1	2	3	4	5	0
(1) Positive attitude to school	1	2	3	4	5	0
(2) Muscular strength and endurance	1	2	3	4	5	0
(3) Ability to persist in the face of difficulties	1	2	3	4	5	0
(4) Awareness of movement themes	1	2	3	4	5	0
(5) Independent thinking	1	2	3	4	5	0
(6) Remedy physical defects	1	2	3	4	5	0
(7) Effective relationships	1	2	3	4	5	0
(8) Motivation to achieve in areas other than physical education	1	2	3	4	5	0
(9) Wide-ranging interests inside and outside school	1	2	3	4	5	0
(10) Cardio-vascular endurance	1	2	3	4	5	0
(11) Ability to communicate through movement	1	2	3	4	5	0
(12) Self-confidence outside the physical education situation	1	2	3	4	5	0
(13) Thinking before taking action	1	2	3	4	5	0
(14) Motor co-ordination	1	2	3	4	5	0
(15) Self-discipline	1	2	3	4	5	0
(16) Enjoyment of participation in physical activity	1	2	3	4	5	0
(17) Ability to take the initiative in a situation	1	2	3	4	5	0

Pupil effects	A great deal		Mod- erate		Little or none	Not sure
	1	2	3	4	5	0
(18) Making allowance for others' deficiencies	1	2	3	4	5	0
(19) Understanding the other's point of view	1	2	3	4	5	0
(20) Positive attitude to authority in general	1	2	3	4	5	0
(21) Motivation to achieve in physical education	1	2	3	4	5	0
(22) Wide range of movement skills	1	2	3	4	5	0
(23) Awareness of one's own deficiencies	1	2	3	4	5	0
(24) General self- confidence	1	2	3	4	5	0
(25) Sense of responsibility	1	2	3	4	5	0
(26) Ability to get on with others	1	2	3	4	5	0
(27) General physical development	1	2	3	4	5	0
(28) Appreciation of limitations and capabilities	1	2	3	4	5	0
(29) Satisfaction from success in physical activity	1	2	3	4	5	0
(30) Release from tensions that develop during school day	1	2	3	4	5	0

Space for additional effects, if any

....

INFLUENCING FACTORS

23. Listed below are some factors which may influence your work as a physical education teacher. If you think a factor is 'very important' circle (1); if you think it is 'not at all important' circle (5); if you think the importance is somewhere between these extremes, circle the appropriate number.

Influencing factors	Very important				Not at all important	Not sure
	1	2	3	4	5	0
(1) Timetabled teaching load involved	1	2	3	4	5	0
(2) Extent of help afforded by non-physical education staff	1	2	3	4	5	0
(3) Special demands made by the school on the physical education teacher because of his/her expertise (injuries, first aid, sports day, etc.)	1	2	3	4	5	0
(4) Diversity of curricular activities	1	2	3	4	5	0
(5) Attitude of school staff to physical education	1	2	3	4	5	0
(6) Adequacy of facilities available for physical education	1	2	3	4	5	0
(7) Recognition from superiors of worthwhile work	1	2	3	4	5	0
(8) Freedom given to the teacher to experiment with different instructional approaches	1	2	3	4	5	0
(9) Extra duties assigned during the school day	1	2	3	4	5	0

Influencing factors	Very im- portant				Not at all im- portant	Not sure
	1	2	3	4	5	0
(10) Number of clerical duties which have to be discharged	1	2	3	4	5	0
(11) A considerable proportion of pupils hostile to 'school'	1	2	3	4	5	0
(12) Legal liability for accidents	1	2	3	4	5	0
(13) Total number of different pupils who have to be taught	1	2	3	4	5	0
(14) 'Intellectually inferior' label sometimes associated with physical education	1	2	3	4	5	0
(15) Difficulty for some pupils in providing the required equipment	1	2	3	4	5	0
(16) Amount of money allotted to physical education for equipment	1	2	3	4	5	0
(17) Problem of 'discipline' in the special physical education situation	1	2	3	4	5	0
(18) Inequitable use of shared facilities	1	2	3	4	5	0
(19) Timetable allocation given to physical education	1	2	3	4	5	0
(20) Range of individual abilities within classes	1	2	3	4	5	0

TEACHER CHARACTERISTICS

24. How important for a successful physical education teacher do you think is each of the following characteristics? Circle the appropriate number.

Characteristics	Very important				Not at all important	Not sure
	1	2	3	4	5	0
(1) Being able to communicate ideas	1	2	3	4	5	0
(2) High standard of honesty and integrity	1	2	3	4	5	0
(3) A thorough knowledge of the subject-matter	1	2	3	4	5	0
(4) A capacity for meticulous attention to details	1	2	3	4	5	0
(5) Extroverted personality	1	2	3	4	5	0
(6) A capacity for sustained hard work	1	2	3	4	5	0
(7) Creative ability	1	2	3	4	5	0
(8) Maturity of outlook	1	2	3	4	5	0
(9) A desire to improve the world or society in some way	1	2	3	4	5	0
(10) A pleasing manner and appearance	1	2	3	4	5	0
(11) Well spoken and well dressed	1	2	3	4	5	0
(12) Ability to gain the respect and confidence of pupils with whom the teacher deals	1	2	3	4	5	0
(13) Having contacts within the teaching professions	1	2	3	4	5	0
(14) Ability to get on well with colleagues	1	2	3	4	5	0
(15) Ability to inspire confidence	1	2	3	4	5	0

Characteristics	Very im- portant				Not at all im- portant	Not sure
	1	2	3	4	5	0
(16) A concern for the interests and well-being of the community	1	2	3	4	5	0
(17) A family background in teaching	1	2	3	4	5	0
(18) A broad cultural knowledge	1	2	3	4	5	0
(19) Administrative ability	1	2	3	4	5	0
(20) A good academic record	1	2	3	4	5	0
(21) A knowledge of recent developments in educational practice	1	2	3	4	5	0
(22) A knowledge of child psychology	1	2	3	4	5	0
(23) Interest in the social background of pupils	1	2	3	4	5	0
(24) Belief in equality of opportunity for everybody	1	2	3	4	5	0

THANK YOU

In a questionnaire of this type it is not possible to ask questions about every topic that may be of importance. If you feel that some important issues concerning the structure and teaching of the physical education programme have been omitted please add a brief note below. [Space left for comments.]

Appendix B   Analysis of teaching styles and gymnastics approach (by age group)

Teaching styles

Teachers estimated on a five-point scale (5 = high) the extent to which they used five teaching styles described as *direct, guided discovery, problem-solving, creative* and *individualised programmes*. In the main body of the report (pp. 46–8) the ranking according to mean value for each teaching style is recorded for the total group of respondents, and for men and women teachers separately. The teaching styles most highly emphasised by the total group of teachers were guided discovery, direct teaching and problem-solving, and these three styles occupied the first three places for both men and women teachers, though the order varied slightly. As the teachers considered that they used these three particular styles of teaching much more often than the other two listed, it was thought appropriate to investigate the way in which these popular styles of teaching might be linked with the age of the teacher.

Consequently the mean scores of each age group (see Q.4, p. 75) on the teaching styles were calculated and assembled in Table B.1. In this table the ranking of each teaching style according to the emphasis placed on it by the respective age groups is also shown. In order to facilitate a comparison of the mean scores for the five age groups on guided discovery, direct teaching and problem-solving, three tables (B.2, B.3 and B.4) show the rankings of the five age groups on these three teaching styles. In general, it would seem from an inspection of the mean scores that differences do exist between the age groups of teachers in the apparent use they make of these styles. A straightforward statistical analysis of these differences is hazardous because of the nature of the data, but in order to add to the interpretation of the observable differences between the means and their ranking, an F-ratio was calculated and is tentatively included.

Table B.1 shows that guided discovery receives the highest rating from four of the five age groups, and that guided discovery, direct teaching and problem-solving in different arrangements occupy the first three places for all five age groups. The fourth and fifth (lowest) ranking of the creative

Table B.1　Teaching style emphasis by age group
(rankings in brackets)

Style		Age group				
		21–22	23–25	26–30	31–39	40 & over
Direct	Mean	3·48 (3)	3·57 (3)	3·71 (2)	3·81 (1)	3·76 (2)
	SD	0·83	0·87	0·84	0·84	0·97
Guided	Mean	4·04 (1)	4·03 (1)	4·00 (1)	3·74 (2)	3·79 (1)
discovery	SD	0·75	0·79	0·87	0·85	0·80
Problem	Mean	3·66 (2)	3·61 (2)	3·43 (3)	3·38 (3)	3·32 (3)
solving	SD	0·80	0·83	0·79	0·91	0·85
Creative	Mean	2·80 (4)	2·59 (4)	2·54 (4)	2·35 (5)	2·43 (4)
	SD	1·10	1·00	0·98	0·92	0·96
ndividualised	Mean	2·23 (5)	2·35 (5)	2·37 (5)	2·44 (4)	2·35 (5)
programmes	SD	0·97	0·97	1·07	0·95	1·06

Table B.2　Mean scores on guided discovery ranked by age group

Rank	Age group	Mean
1	21–22	4·04
2	23–25	4·03
3	26–30	4·00
4	40 & over	3·79
5	31–39	3·74

The F-ratio 5·3199 is significant.

approach and the individualised programme approach is confirmed in four of the five age groups.

Table B.2 reveals that the two oldest groups of teachers put a considerably lower emphasis on guided discovery than the three younger groups. In general, the trend is for less importance to be placed on this style of teaching as the age of the group increases.

From an inspection of the means in Table B.3 the interpretation would seem to be that the youngest two teacher groups are distinguished from the three older groups in placing less emphasis on the direct teaching approach. The difference between the mean scores of the lowest ranked group and the highest ranked approximates to half a standard deviation.

Table B.3 Mean scores on direct teaching ranked by age group

Rank	Age group	Mean
1	31–39	3·81
2	40 & over	3·76
3	26–30	3·71
4	23–25	3·57
5	21–22	3·48

The F-ratio 4·133 is significant.

Table B.4 Mean scores on problem-solving ranked by age group

Rank	Age group	Mean
1	21–22	3·66
2	23–25	3·61
3	26–30	3·43
4	31–39	3·38
5	40 & over	3·32

The F-ratio 4·609 is significant.

For the teaching style described as problem-solving, Table B.4 shows a decreasing emphasis with the increasing age of the groups. The main difference seems to be between the two oldest groups and the three younger groups.

Summary
The extent to which teachers use the five listed styles of teaching appears to be related to their age. A comparison of the mean scores for the five age groups of teachers on the three most popular teaching styles confirmed this view. Younger teachers emphasised guided discovery and problem-solving styles considerably more and direct teaching considerably less than older groups of teachers.

Approaches to gymnastics

Approximately 94% of all respondents teach gymnastics. These teachers were asked to estimate the use they made of certain principles of learning and teaching, which derive from psychology, physiology, mechanics and movement theory. The relative emphasis placed by teachers on the five approach principles are given in the main body of the report (see pp. 48–50). The most popular of these were clearly *lead-up stages*, *learning 'principles'* and *movement 'principles'*. This section reports in summary on a small extension of the main survey in which these three relatively popular approaches to the teaching of gymnastics are linked with the age of the teachers. The mean scores for each of the three approaches are compared in Tables B.5, B.6 and B.7. The means are ranked in order and an interpretation of the ranking is subjectively made. The possible significance of differences between mean scores is tentatively assessed from the F-ratios.

Table B.5   Mean scores on lead-up stages ranked by age group

Rank	Age group	Mean
1	40 & over	4·25
2	21–22	4·17
3	23–25	4·05
4	31–39	4·02
5	26–30	3·97

The F-ratio 1·798 is not significant.

There appears to be no relationship between emphasis on lead-up stages and the age of the teacher. While the oldest group of teachers occupies the highest rank the youngest group fills the second rank with a similar mean score.

Table B.6   Mean scores on learning 'principles' ranked by age group

Rank	Age group	Mean
1	21–22	3·76
2	23–25	3·64
3	26–30	3·58
4	40 & over	3·55
5	31–39	3·45

The F-ratio 2·095 is not significant.

Table B.6 shows that the youngest teacher groups place greatest emphasis on the use of learning principles. The two oldest groups occupy the last two ranks, indicating that they make less use of these teaching principles.

The distinction to be drawn from the mean scores shown in Table B.7 is between the three younger groups of teachers, with mean scores in excess of 4·0 (indicating that they often apply movement 'principles'), and the two oldest (thirty-plus) groups. It may be that this apparent difference between those under thirty and those over in terms of emphasis placed on a

Table B.7 Mean scores on movement 'principles' ranked by age group

Rank	Age group	Mean
1	23–25	4·08
2	21–22	4·06
3	26–30	4·01
4	40 & over	3·73
5	31–39	3·71

The *F*-ratio 5·407 is significant.

movement approach to gymnastics teaching is linked with their initial training.

Summary

No systematic link between the age of the teachers and the extent of their use of lead-up stages in teaching gymnastics is evident. Younger teachers tend to make more use of psychological principles of learning than older (over thirty) teachers, though the real significance of the difference is to be interpreted with caution. However, age does seem to be related to the use made of movement 'principles'. Older teachers had substantially lower mean scores than younger teachers, indicating that they use a movement approach considerably less often.

Appendix C Factor analysis of pupil effects, influencing factors and teacher characteristics

In order to ascertain the main element in teachers' responses to items concerning their perceptions of pupil effects (30 items), influencing factors (20 items), and teacher characteristics (24 items), three component analyses were carried out from the intercorrelations, using the University of London computer program BMD03M. In each case seven factors were rotated to an orthogonal solution according to the Varimax criterion.

The analyses summarised below are reported in full in Tables C.1, C.8 and C.15.

(a) *Pupil effects:* Seven rotated factors were produced and named to explain the major elements in the teachers' thirty responses. Those seven factors accounted for approximately 56% of the variance.

(b) *Influencing factors:* Seven factors were rotated and named to explain the major elements in the teachers' perception of twenty items which appear to influence their teaching. These seven factors accounted for 56% of the variance.

(c) *Teacher characteristics:* Seven factors accounting for 53% of the variance were rotated to explain teachers' views of twenty-four personal characteristics necessary for success in teaching.

Factor scores were computed for each individual on the first three factors in each of the three analyses (University of London Fortap computer program) and these scaled scores were analysed separately for:

(i) men and women respondents;
(ii) the five age groups of respondents (see Q.4, p. 75).

Pupil effects (Part III, Q.22, pp. 80–2).

Interpretation of factors
Table C.1 lists the thirty items and their rotated loadings on the seven factors. The seven factors were identified and named from the loadings.

Factor i: High loadings are shown on variables 18 and 19, and moderate loadings on variables 20, 25 and 26. These loadings appear meaningful in relating variables which describe awareness of the other's point of view and

Table C.1 Pupil effects: variables and rotated component loadings

Variable	Component loadings*						
	i	ii	iii	iv	v	vi	vii
(1) Positive attitude to school	05	09	05	−06	**60**	17	14
(2) Muscular strength and endurance	02	**84**	11	−10	05	−03	06
(3) Ability to persist in face of difficulties	34	36	−07	08	17	−02	43
(4) Awareness of movement themes	17	04	09	**82**	01	−03	05
(5) Independent thinking	26	−04	04	46	23	−11	**48**
(6) Remedy physical defects	11	**57**	−04	26	19	−14	03
(7) Effective relationships	31	13	15	01	**42**	−24	24
(8) Motivation to achieve in areas other than PE	29	05	−15	18	**55**	−07	15
(9) Wide-ranging interests inside and outside school	23	12	08	23	**61**	07	−11
(10) Cardio-vascular endurance	−02	**82**	13	−08	09	02	15
(11) Ability to communicate movement	−10	31	19	17	19	−49	30
(12) Self-confidence outside the PE situation	01	05	29	−09	**56**	−02	45
(13) Thinking before taking action	27	09	00	12	09	−06	**73**
(14) Motor co-ordination	−02	37	26	32	−11	15	48
(15) Self-discipline	36	10	11	03	13	21	**62**
(16) Enjoyment of participation in physical activity	08	16	16	01	21	68	19
(17) Ability to take the initiative in a situation	38	11	06	05	26	06	**50**
(18) Making allowances for others' deficiencies	**74**	01	20	14	−01	03	13
(19) Understanding the other's point of view	**77**	−05	08	11	14	−01	20
(20) Positive attitude to authority in general	**49**	15	07	−06	33	17	15
(21) Motivation to achieve in PE	−11	02	**58**	32	37	06	01
(22) Wide range of movement skills	−08	19	**45**	**59**	09	02	21
(23) Awareness of one's own deficiences	31	09	**67**	−02	−10	−21	02
(24) General self-confidence	22	14	**35**	−07	38	08	39
(25) Sense of responsibility	**49**	08	13	00	38	01	31
(26) Ability to get on with others	**54**	07	19	03	29	09	23
(27) General physical development	12	**68**	22	10	03	31	09

* Decimal point omitted; loadings rounded to two places.

Table C.1—*cont.*

Variable	Component loadings*						
	i	ii	iii	iv	v	vi	vii
(28) Appreciation of limitations and capabilities	37	11	**64**	01	−11	−16	16
(29) Satisfaction from success in physical activity	01	09	**60**	05	21	36	10
(30) Release from tensions that develop during school day	11	11	46	13	08	12	01
Cumulative % variance	25·2	33·2	39·1	44·2	48·8	52·4	55·8

general responsibility. The factor is therefore named *social awareness and responsibility.*

Factor ii: The interpretation of this factor is straightforward, due to the way in which the high (variables 2 and 10) and moderate (variables 6 and 27) loadings are clearly linked with physical and organic development. The factor therefore describes *general physical development.*

Factor iii: The interpretation of this factor is difficult. While the two highest loadings (variables 23 and 28) are indicative of a realistic self-awareness, moderate loadings point to the involvement in physical education developing motivation to achieve (variable 21) and related satisfaction (variable 29). The way in which self-awareness is associated with motivation and satisfaction is not clear from the loadings in general but the association is plausible. The factor is named *self-awareness.*

Factor iv: With the only high loadings on the variables describing movement skills and awareness (variables 4 and 22), this factor appears to describe *general movement ability.*

Factor v: Moderately high loadings (variables 1 and 9) describe positive attitude to and interest in school. The only other important loadings (variables 7 and 8) support this interpretation, indicating a positive approach to education. The factor is named *general interest in school.*

Factor vi: This factor is not clear from the loadings but appears to describe *enjoyment in physical activity.*

Factor vii: The high and moderate loadings (variables 13, 15, 17 and 5) appear to be related in describing general cognitive ability which is linked with a practical outcome. The factor is therefore named *cognitive judgement.*

Analysis of factor scores by sex and age
In order to investigate possible sex differences in the teachers' views of the effects of the physical education programme, factor scores on the three

largest and most important factors were computed separately for men and women (University of London computer program BMD07D). The mean scores and standard deviations on each of the three factors for the total group of teachers, for men and for women are shown in Tables C.2, C.3 and C.4, together with an analysis of the significance of the different results for men and women.

Table C.2 Mean scores on factor i, social awareness and responsibility: analysis men v. women

	Men (n = 455)	Women (n = 433)
Mean	15·45	15·11
SD	4·56	4·52

Analysis of variance: F-ratio 1·276 not significant.

The mean scores for men and women teachers on factor i are clearly similar, the difference between them being non-significant. The interpretation of this analysis is that men and women teachers do not differ in the importance they ascribe to the dimension described as social awareness and responsibility.

Table C.3 Mean scores on factor ii, general physical development: analysis men v. women

	Men (n = 455)	Women (n = 433)
Mean	14·95	16·36
SD	4·63	4·69

Analysis of variance

	S.s.*	D.f.†	Mean s.‡	F-ratio	Significance
Between	443·0516	1	443·0516	20·437	0·001
Within	19 207·9113	886	21·6794		
TOTAL	19 650·9629	887			

* Sum of squares   † Degrees of freedom   ‡ Mean square

The mean factor score for women is substantially higher than for men and the difference is highly significant. The women teachers in the sample are apparently more strongly convinced than the men that general physical development is brought about by involvement in physical education.

Table C.4 Mean scores on factor iii, self-awareness: analysis men v. women

	Men (n = 455)	Women (n = 433)
Men	16·59	16·82
SD	5·21	5·18

Analysis of variance: F-ratio 0·4133 not significant.

There is no significant difference between men and women teachers' mean scores on the factor described as self-awareness.

In another series of analyses, the relationship between the age of teachers and their factor scores was investigated. The teachers were divided into five age groups (see Q.4, p. 75) and the mean factor scores for the groups subjected to analysis of variance. The summary statistics are shown in Tables C.5, C.6 and C.7.

Table C.5 Mean scores on factor i, social awareness and responsibility: analysis by age groups

	Age group				
	21–22 (n = 120)	23–25 (n = 291)	26–30 (n = 185)	31–39 (n = 190)	40 & over (n = 102)
Mean	16·48	15·08	15·04	15·74	14·03
SD	4·34	4·01	4·55	4·96	4·99

Analysis of variance:

	S.s.	D.f.	Mean s.	F-ratio	Significance
Between	396·0556	4	99·0139	4·8870	0·01
Within	17 889·9973	883	20·2605		
TOTAL	18 286·0529	887			

The youngest group of teachers has the highest mean score and the oldest group the lowest mean score on this factor. This is clearly the largest inter-group difference and accounts for the significant F-ratio. This result is interpreted as indicating that there is a difference among teachers according to age in the emphasis they place on social awareness and responsibility. Younger teachers rate this outcome significantly higher than older teachers.

Table C.6 Mean scores on factor ii, general physical development: analysis by age groups

	Age group				
	21–22 (n = 120)	23–25 (n = 291)	26–30 (n = 185)	31–39 (n = 190)	40 & over (n = 102)
Mean	16·83	15·73	15·47	15·44	14·69
SD	4·60	4·57	4·72	4·65	5·09

Analysis of variance:

	S.s.	D.f.	Mean s.	F-ratio	Significance
Between	276·9065	4	69·2266	3·1551	0·05
Within	19 374·0564	883	21·9412		
TOTAL	19 650·9629	887			

The mean scores show a clear trend with age, the older groups having lower mean scores. The biggest difference is between the youngest group, who rate this factor highest, and the oldest group, who rate it significantly lower.

Table C.7 Mean scores on factor iii, self-awareness: analysis by age groups

	Age group				
	21–22 (n = 120)	23–25 (n = 291)	26–30 (n = 185)	31–39 (n = 190)	40 & over (n = 102)
Mean	17·52	16·38	16·61	16·74	16·75
SD	5·12	4·99	5·09	5·30	5·76

Analysis of variance: F-ratio 1·0381 not significant.

Although the youngest group of teachers has the highest mean score, there is no other trend with age and no inter-group difference reaches the level of significance.

Summary

The teachers' emphases in response to the items on thirty pupil effects were factor analysed, and seven factors accounting for 56% of the variance were identified and described. Factor scores for each individual on the three largest factors were computed. A comparison of factor scores by sex and age was undertaken. When men teachers' scores were compared with women's, a significant difference was demonstrated on factor ii, general physical development. Significant differences were also found between age groups on factor i, social awareness and responsibility, and on factor ii, general physical development.

Influencing factors (Part III, Q.23, pp. 83–4)

Interpretation of factors

The twenty questionnaire items and their loadings on the seven abstracted factors are listed in Table C.8. The interpretations and factor names are based on the loadings.

Table C.8　Influencing factors: variables and rotated component loadings

Variable	Component loadings*						
	i	ii	iii	iv	v	vi	vii
(1) Timetabled teaching load involved	**54**	01	37	03	11	−24	19
(2) Extent of help afforded by non-PE staff	19	−07	**48**	**−53**	30	01	−03
(3) Special demands made by the school on the PE teacher because of his/her expertise (injuries, first aid, sports day, etc.)	24	05	06	−08	**77**	90	−06
(4) Diversity of curricular activities	**32**	18	27	28	**38**	−09	−05
(5) Attitude of school staff to PE	25	−14	37	05	13	**42**	08
(6) Adequacy of facilities available for PE	−05	22	**64**	07	−11	28	−04
(7) Recognition from superiors of worthwhile work	07	−01	18	11	07	**74**	05

* Decimal point omitted; loadings rounded to two places.

Table C.8—*cont.*

Variable	Component loadings*						
	i	ii	iii	iv	v	vi	vii
(8) Freedom given to experiment with different instructional approaches	15	07	15	**68**	09	14	04
(9) Extra duties assigned during the school day	**75**	−03	−10	00	−01	17	14
(10) Number of clerical duties which have to be discharged	**73**	06	07	06	15	19	02
(11) A considerable proportion of pupils hostile to 'school'	25	14	−10	−08	−04	24	**53**
(12) Legal liability for accidents	−11	04	03	08	**62**	22	39
(13) Total number of different pupils who have to be taught	12	**68**	13	−06	12	−02	28
(14) 'Intellectually inferior' label sometimes associated with PE	10	13	00	−05	12	**63**	27
(15) Difficult for some pupils to provide the required equipment	12	19	09	−36	12	22	**47**
(16) Amount of money allotted to PE for equipment	03	12	**72**	02	13	08	17
(17) Problem of 'discipline' in the special PE situation	−09	18	00	10	36	07	**62**
(18) Inequitable use of shared facilities	13	−03	22	09	−04	05	**70**
(19) Timetable allocation given to PE	06	−09	**44**	39	03	−05	45
(20) Range of individual abilities within classes	−05	**84**	−01	10	02	07	−01
Cumulative % variance	19·3	27·2	33·9	39·9	45·7	51·1	56·2

Factor i : The highest loadings are shown for extra duties and for the number of clerical duties (variables 9 and 10), while the formal timetable load (variable 1) also contributes substantially to this factor. A minor loading on diversity of curricular activities seems to be important for interpretation. The factor appears to reflect both the formal curriculum load that teachers carry and the extra duties expected of them. The factor is named *total work commitment.*

Factor ii: The loadings on this factor show the emphasis to be on the range of pupil abilities (variable 20) and on the total number of different pupils in classes (variable 13). As no other variable seems to be involved in a major way, this factor is described as *diversity of pupils.*

Factor iii: This factor seems to be describable in terms of resources for teaching. The high loadings on variables 16 and 6 emphasise the adequacy of equipment and facilities, and two moderate loadings (variables 2 and 19) indicate related aspects of staffing and timetable resources. The factor is named *resources.*

Factor iv: The highest loading is on variable 8, freedom to experiment with different instructional approaches. The moderately high *negative* loading on variable 2 is difficult to interpret in the context of a liberal atmosphere for teaching, as is the positive relationship with variable 19. The factor is tentatively described as *liberal atmosphere.*

Factor v: The two high loadings on variables 3 and 12 appear to be related to safety problems, about which the teahcer of physical education is specially concerned. The diversity of activities in physical education can contribute to the special safety problem; the minor loading on variable 4 may be seen from this point of view. The factor is named *safety.*

Factor vi: This factor is apparently concerned with attitudes of others to physical education. The high loadings on variables 7 and 14 and the moderate loading on variable 5 would seem to confirm this. The factor is identified as *attitude of colleagues.*

Factor vii: Although the highest loading is on variable 18, this factor would seem to be best interpreted by considering the other three moderately high loadings, which seem to be more clearly related. Variables 17, 11 and 15 are concerned with items which may be basic to problems of discipline. The factor is therefore named *discipline.*

Analysis of factor scores by sex and age

When the factor scores for men and women teachers were compared on factor i, *total work commitment,* no significant difference was observed. Table C.9 shows the mean scores for the two groups to be similar.

Table C.9 Mean scores on factor i, total work commitment: analysis men v. women

	Men ($n = 455$)	Women ($n = 433$)
Mean	14·22	14·15
SD	4·35	4·52

Analysis of variance: F-ratio 0·055 not significant.

There was also no significant difference between men and women on factor ii, diversity of pupils. The statistics are reported in Table C.10.

Table C.10 Mean scores on factor ii, diversity of pupils:
analysis men v. women

	Men ($n = 455$)	Women ($n = 433$)
Mean	14·41	13·97
SD	4·08	4·34

Analysis of variance: F-ratio 2·512 not significant.

On the third factor regarded by teachers as influencing their effectiveness, namely resources, women teachers had a significantly higher mean score than men. It appears, therefore, that women physical education teachers, compared with their male colleagues, consider that resources available have a greater effect on their work. Table C.11 summarises the descriptive statistics and analyses the differences between the groups.

Table C.11 Mean scores on factor iii, resources:
analysis men v. women

	Men ($n = 455$)	Women ($n = 433$)
Mean	10·72	11·73
SD	3·38	3·81

Analysis of variance:

	S.s.	D.f.	Mean s.	F-ratio	Significance
Between	223·7732	1	223·7732	17·3037	0·001
Within	11 457·8473	886	12·9321		
TOTAL	11 681·6205	887			

The way in which the age of the teachers is linked with their scores on the three major influencing factors was investigated by comparing the mean scores for the age groups of teachers (see Q.4, p. 75). The analyses are summarised in Tables C.12–14.

The analysis of the mean scores of the groups shown in Table C.12 indicates that there are no significant differences attributable to the age of the teachers. The view that total work commitment influences teaching is in general equally held by teachers in the five age groups.

Table C.12   Mean scores on factor i, total work commitment: analysis by age groups

	Age group				
	21–22 (n = 120)	23–25 (n = 291)	26–30 (n = 185)	31–39 (n = 190)	40 & over (n = 102)
Mean	14·78	14·37	13·91	13·84	14·01
SD	4·12	4·18	4·41	4·53	5·25

Analysis of variance: F-ratio 1·1506 not significant.

Table C.13   Mean scores on factor ii, diversity of pupils: analysis by age group

	Age group				
	21–22 (n = 120)	23–25 (n = 291)	26–30 (n = 185)	31–39 (n = 190)	40 & over (n = 102)
Mean	13·73	13·92	14·12	14·91	14·34
SD	3·99	3·95	4·13	4·26	5·09

Analysis of variance: F-ratio 2·0832 not significant.

Table C.14   Mean scores on factor iii, resources: analysis by age groups

	Age group				
	21–22 (n = 120)	23–25 (n = 291)	26–30 (n = 185)	31–39 (n = 190)	40 & over (n = 102)
Mean	12·00	11·44	10·64	10·96	11·11
SD	3·93	3·53	3·41	3·39	4·15

Analysis of variance:

	S.s.	D.f.	Mean s.	F-ratio	Significance
Between	162·7962	4	40·6990	3·1199	0·05
Within	11 518·2021	883	13 0451		
TOTAL	11 681·9983	887			

Although the two youngest age groups of teachers have lower mean scores than the three older groups, the differences do not reach significant levels. It appears that teachers of all age groups strongly believe diversity of pupils is one of the major influences on their work.

The youngest group of teachers has the highest mean factor score on factor iii, resources. It would seem that they are more convinced than others who have had longer experience that the resources available affect them in their teaching duties.

Summary
The teachers' ratings of the importance they attributed to the twenty items describing influences which might affect their work were factor analysed. Seven factors accounting for 56% of the total variance were abstracted and described. A comparison of factor scores by sex and age on the three largest factors was undertaken. On factor i, total work commitment, or on factor ii, diversity of pupils, no significant difference was found, either between the men and women, or between the five age groups. A highly significant difference was, however, identified between men and women on factor iii, resources, indicating that women regard this influencing factor more highly than men. Age was also found to be related to scores on factor iii, the youngest group of teachers having the highest mean score.

Teacher characteristics (Part III, Q.24, pp. 85–6)

Interpretation of factors
The factor analysis computed on the twenty-four items of the teacher characteristics questionnaire is summarised in Table C.15. The loadings on the seven abstracted factors and the contribution of these factors to the total variance is shown.

Factor i: This large factor, accounting for 22% of personal characteristics and dispositions important for a successful physical education teacher, appears to emphasise the individual's general educational background. Highest loadings are on a good academic record (variable 20) and on a broad cultural background (variable 18). A moderately high loading is shown on a knowledge of recent developments in educational practice (variable 21), which is in keeping with the general interpretation of a well-educated and knowledgeable individual. The minor loadings on variables 11, 10 and 22, add a dimension of professional knowledge and orientation to the interpretation of this factor, which is described as *personal education*.

Factor ii: The interpretation of this factor seems to be best approached by considering the moderately high loadings on the related variables 9 and 16, which together describe a disposition of concern for others, and for society at large. This social altruism dimension is linked in this factor with maturity

Table C.15 Teacher characteristics: variables and rotated component loadings

Variable	Component loadings*						
	i	ii	iii	iv	v	vi	vii
(1) Being able to communicate ideas	09	−04	**56**	−08	03	09	40
(2) High standard of honesty and integrity	09	**54**	**47**	−06	13	−10	08
(3) A thorough knowledge of the subject matter	10	−13	08	12	09	01	**58**
(4) A capacity for meticulous attention to details	23	31	07	−02	25	04	**53**
(5) Extroverted personality	−11	−02	03	13	08	**67**	31
(6) A capacity for sustained hard work	−07	22	16	10	38	−02	**44**
(7) Creative ability	04	40	02	20	−11	11	**54**
(8) Maturity of outlook	11	**64**	11	12	21	−06	16
(9) A desire to improve the world or society in some way	13	**59**	−08	25	07	33	−02
(10) A pleasing manner and appearance	25	36	41	04	11	−04	19
(11) Well spoken and well dressed	38	−25	40	10	40	**40**	−10
(12) Ability to gain the respect and confidence of pupils with whom the teacher deals	−05	16	**70**	24	−04	−01	−10
(13) Having contacts within the teaching professions	04	12	−02	12	**61**	22	06
(14) Ability to get on well with colleagues	10	16	16	20	**64**	07	07
(15) Ability to inspire confidence	−04	05	**51**	26	29	01	22
(16) A concern for the interests and well-being of community	10	**55**	19	34	20	24	−06
(17) A family background in teaching	17	14	−01	−05	−02	**60**	−10
(18) A broad cultural knowledge	**64**	36	−01	15	18	02	05
(19) Administrative ability	16	09	03	06	**71**	−21	12
(20) A good academic record	**73**	11	03	06	13	11	20
(21) A knowledge of recent developments in educational practice	50	−02	10	**50**	−07	01	25
(22) A knowledge of child psychology	25	05	08	**70**	07	−06	11
(23) Interest in social background of pupils	02	18	10	**70**	18	01	03
(24) Belief in equality of opportunity for everybody	−03	15	07	**64**	17	13	07
Cumulative % variance	22·0	28·1	33·6	38·9	43·9	48·6	53·0

* Decimal point omitted; loadings rounded to two places.

of outlook (variable 8), and this relationship might seem to have a good deal of face validity. The factor is named *social concern.*

Factor iii: The three highest loadings on this factor describe teacher qualities and abilities that are concerned with establishing good relationships with pupils. Ability to gain their respect and confidence (variable 12) has the largest emphasis and the abilities to communicate and to inspire confidence (variables 1 and 15) would seem to be clearly related to the central meaning of the factor. The moderately high loading on variable 2 places a minor emphasis on the teacher's honesty and integrity, characteristics which would surely facilitate the development of respect, confidence and good interpersonal communication. The factor may be described as *rapport.*

Factor iv: This factor is described by the high loadings on variables 21–23. These refer in general to knowledge about children—child psychology (variable 22), social background (variable 23), and modern educational practices suitable for them (variable 21). The loading on variable 24 is not unrelated to the main emphasis of this factor, which is described as *knowledge of children.*

Factor v: The high loadings on this factor link administrative ability (variable 19) with ability to get on well with colleagues (variable 14) and having contacts within the teaching profession (variable 13). Together these seem to describe two aspects of professional organisation: awareness and involvement. The factor is named *professional organisation.*

Factor vi: Extroverted personality (variable 5) has the highest loading on this factor, in which it is related to a family background in teaching and being well spoken and well dressed (variables 17 and 11). Taken together, these three interrelated items appear to describe a disposition of self-assurance which would be a reasonable characteristic for the successful teacher. The factor is therefore named *assurance.*

Factor vii: The main loadings on this factor draw attention to thorough application (variables 4 and 6), knowledge of the subject (variable 3) and creativity (variable 7). It may be that the factor describes the enlightened conscientiousness of the successful teacher. The factor is tentatively named *application* to reflect the major emphasis.

Analysis of factor scores by sex and age
The three analyses comparing the factor scores of men and women revealed no significant differences.

The analysis of scores on factor i, personal education, is shown in Table C.16. The mean scores are seen to be similar, with the *F*-ratio for the difference not approaching a significant level.

On this major characteristic describing personal education, therefore, men and women teachers do not differ greatly in the importance they ascribe to it.

The scores on factor ii, social concern, are also similar for men and women

Table C.16   Mean scores on factor i, personal education:
analysis men v. women

	Men (n = 455)	Women (n = 433)
Mean	14·63	14·37
SD	4·06	3·75

Analysis of variance: F-ratio 0·9743 not significant.

teachers, indicating that they do not differ significantly as groups in the
importance they attach to social concern as a characteristic necessary for
success in teaching. The analysis of the group scores is summarised in
Table C.17 and shows a non-significant *F*-ratio.

Table C.17   Mean scores on factor ii, social concern:
analysis men v. women

	Men (n = 455)	Women (n = 433)
Mean	12·88	12·75
SD	3·80	3·52

Analysis of variance: F-ratio 0·2830 not significant.

On the third teacher characteristic, described as rapport, again no significant difference was observed between the factor scores of men and women.
The interpretation is that men and women teachers of physical education
equally consider it important that the successful teacher must be able to
establish appropriate rapport. Table C.18 summarises the details of the
analysis and shows the observed non-significant *F*-ratio.

Table C.18   Mean scores on factor iii, rapport:
analysis men v. women

	Men (n = 455)	Women (n = 433)
Mean	10·50	10·56
SD	3·43	3·09

Analysis of variance: F-ratio 0·0746 not significant.

In the three analyses of factor scores by age significant differences were revealed. The mean scores for the age groups on factor i, personal education, show a clear trend with age. From Table C.19, the greatest difference may be seen to be between the youngest and the oldest teachers.

Table C.19 Mean scores on factor i, personal education: analysis by age groups

	Age group				
	21–22 ($n = 120$)	23–25 ($n = 291$)	26–30 ($n = 185$)	31–39 ($n = 190$)	40 & over ($n = 102$)
Mean	15·42	14·98	14·21	14·14	13·26
SD	3·49	3·97	3·75	4·07	3·80

Analysis of variance:

	S.s.	D.f.	Mean s.	*F*-ratio	Significance
Between	364·6876	4	91·1719	6·0982	0·01
Within	13 201·3124	883			
TOTAL	13 566·0000	887			

Table C.20 Mean scores on factor ii, social concern: analysis by age groups

	Age group				
	21–22 ($n = 120$)	23–25 ($n = 291$)	26–30 ($n = 185$)	31–39 ($n = 190$)	40 & over ($n = 102$)
Mean	14·12	12·96	12·63	12·47	11·78
SD	3·75	3·77	3·73	3·34	3·32

Analysis of variance:

	S.s.	D.f.	Mean s.	*F*-ratio	Significance
Between	354·1639	4	88·5410	6·7615	0·01
Within	11 562·8046	883	13·0949		
TOTAL	11 916·9685	887			

The youngest teachers had the highest mean score, indicating that compared with the oldest teachers they held a significantly stronger view that personal education was of primary importance for the successful physical educationist.

On factor ii, social concern, the age group scores again show a clear-cut trend with age. Again the highest mean score is found for the youngest group of teachers. The mean scores and the highly significant differences between them are given in Table C.20.

The F-ratio of the differences between groups is shown as highly significant, due largely to the relatively high mean score of the youngest teachers and the very low mean score of the oldest group. The largest difference between these two groups is interpreted as demonstrating that the youngest teachers, compared with the oldest, emphasise the importance of social concern for the successful teacher.

The differences between the mean scores on factor iii, rapport, are smaller than those observed on the first and second factors. A significant difference is found, but only at the lower 0·05 level. The largest difference is between the youngest teachers, whose mean score is highest, and those aged between 31 and 39, who have the lowest mean score. Table C.21 gives a summary of the statistics and details of the analysis.

Table C.21   Mean scores on factor iii, rapport: analysis by age groups

	Age group				
	21–22 $(n = 120)$	23–25 $(n = 291)$	26–30 $(n = 185)$	31–39 $(n = 190)$	40 & over $(n = 102)$
Mean	11·27	10·73	10·28	10·10	10·34
SD	3·29	3·29	3·32	3·02	3·38

Analysis of variance:

	S.s.	D.f.	Mean s.	F-ratio	Significance
Between	128·5112	4	32·1278	3·0338	0·05
Within	9 350·7849	883	10·5898		
TOTAL	9 479·2961	887			

It appears from this analysis that the ability to establish rapport is regarded as of significantly higher importance by the youngest teachers compared with their older colleagues.

Summary
The ratings given by teachers to the twenty-four items describing the personal characteristics they believed to be important for the successful physical education teacher were factor analysed. Seven factors, accounting for 53% of the total variance, were identified and described. A comparison of factor scores by sex and age on the three largest factors was undertaken. No differences were found between men and women teachers on the factors. Significant differences were found, however, between the five age groups on all three factors. In each case the youngest teachers had the highest mean scores.

Appendix D Activity emphasis in years 1–5 of secondary schools

Table D.1 Activity emphasis in boys' and girls' physical education departments based on a six-point (1 = high) scale

	Boys	Mean	SD	Girls	Mean	SD
Year 1	Team games	1·4	0·9	Team games	1·6	1·0
	Gymnastics	2·3	1·1	Gymnastics	2·0	1·1
	Athletics	3·0	0·9	Swimming	3·2	1·4
	Swimming	3·1	1·0	Athletics	3·4	1·2
	Outdoor pursuits	4·7	1·1	Dance	3·5	1·5
	Dance	5·1	0·9	Outdoor pursuits	5·2	1·3
Year 2	Team games	1·3	0·7	Team games	1·4	0·8
	Gymnastics	2·3	1·1	Gymnastics	2·0	1·1
	Athletics	2·8	0·9	Athletics	3·3	1·1
	Swimming	3·2	1·1	Swimming	3·4	1·3
	Outdoor pursuits	4·6	1·1	Dance	3·5	1·4
	Dance	5·2	0·9	Outdoor pursuits	5·2	1·3
Year 3	Team games	1·2	0·7	Team games	1·4	0·8
	Gymnastics	2·6	1·0	Gymnastics	2·2	1·1
	Athletics	2·7	0·9	Athletics	3·0	1·1
	Swimming	3·3	1·2	Swimming	3·4	1·3
	Outdoor pursuits	4·2	1·2	Dance	3·5	1·4
	Dance	5·3	0·9	Outdoor pursuits	4·7	1·5
Year 4	Team games	1·2	0·6	Team games	1·3	0·8
	Athletics	2·5	0·8	Gymnastics	2·6	1·2
	Gymnastics	3·0	1·1	Athletics	2·8	1·1
	Swimming	3·4	1·2	Swimming	3·4	1·4
	Outdoor pursuits	3·8	1·2	Dance	3·7	1·5
	Dance	5·3	0·8	Outdoor pursuits	4·0	1·7
Year 5	Team games	1·2	0·7	Team games	1·3	0·9
	Athletics	2·5	0·7	Gymnastics	2·8	1·3
	Gymnastics	3·1	1·2	Athletics	2·9	1·1
	Swimming	3·2	1·2	Dance	3·2	1·5
	Outdoor pursuits	3·5	1·4	Swimming	3·3	1·5
	Dance	5·3	0·9	Outdoor pursuits	3·6	1·8

Appendix E Physical education in boys' public schools (mostly boarding)

B. Ashley, Director of Physical Education, Marlborough College

The original questionnaires designed for the enquiry were found by the small number of independent school respondents to be inappropriate in various ways. In response to Dr Kane's request for more information on the details of physical education in independent schools, the original questionnaire was modified and distributed to fifty independent boarding schools (representing a one-in-four sample of those schools with over 200 boarders).

It was hoped that the response would throw more light, in particular, on:

(a) the average class time for ·physical education allocated in independent schools;

(b) objectives of the physical education programme;

(c) teacher profiles.

There were forty-three completed returns from boarding schools in England with a range of 279–900 pupils (nearly all aged thirteen to eighteen).

Average class time (ACT)

There were many difficulties in the way of finding out the average class time (see pp. 3–4) for physical education. In many schools there were games afternoons for the whole school and in no school did there seem to be a shortage of facilities for outdoor team games. As tradition dictated that there was a time for working and a time for playing, most schools were able to exercise all their pupils at the same time.

However, some kind of comparison with state schools was attempted by ascertaining:

(a) the time devoted to physical education in the timetable when other subjects were being taught;

(b) time devoted to compulsory games;

(c) time spent on voluntary games.

As may be expected, there were very wide discrepancies—it is a pity that no comparable evidence from state boarding schools was available. Most schools had between one and two periods of approximately 40 minutes each of timetabled physical education up to O level; the ACT for the total of independent schools responding ($n = 43$) was 60 minutes. Some schools had timetabled physical education throughout the school career from thirteen to eighteen.

GAMES TIME

   (a) *Compulsory:* This ranged from zero (at a music school) to $8\frac{1}{2}$ hours per week. There was a gradual lessening in compulsion over the years, but thirteen-year-olds averaged 260 minutes and in only a few schools had compulsory games finished by the sixth form. ('Games' must be interpreted very widely—for example, one school insisted on compulsory exercise and offered beagling as an option.)

   (b) *Voluntary:* The estimated average for the schools was about two hours per week, though in most schools boys could spend up to five or six afternoons on games.

   (c) *Total games time:* Excluding timetabled physical education, the average time spent on games was $6\frac{1}{2}$ to 7 hours per week. Two schools estimated 11 hours per week.

The overall ACT (including physical education periods in the timetable) was 450 minutes per week for the years up to O level.

Conclusion

As part of their normal school curriculum, boys in independent boarding schools spent more than three times the time on physical education (including games) that their counterparts in state schools did, though doubtless many boys in state schools supplement their physical education with games or youth clubs in the evenings and weekends.

Table E.1 Comparison of objectives between men teachers in independent and state schools ($n = 43$ and 455)

Independent schools			State schools		
Rank	Objective	Mean	Rank	Objective	Mean
1	Organic development	2·971	1	Leisure	3·490
2	Motor skills	3·171	2	Motor skills	3·649
3	Self-realisation	3·257	3	Self-realisation	3·686
4	Leisure	3·285	4	Organic development	4·601
5=	Social competence	5·340	5	Moral development	4·613
5=	Moral development	5·340	6	Emotional stability	4·773
7	Emotional stability	5·914	7	Social competence	5·373
8	Cognitive development	6·685	8	Cognitive development	6·459
9	Aesthetic appreciation	7·340	9	Aesthetic appreciation	7·188

Objectives

In view of the findings for average class time, one would have expected some differences in the objectives of the teachers. Table E.1 illustrates the comparison between men teachers in independent and state schools in their ranking of the nine objectives in Part III, question 15 (see pp. 76–7).

Pupil effects

Tables E.2 and E.3 show the ranking of the highest and lowest items in Part III, question 22 (see pp. 80–2). The third highest rank is seen to be muscular strength and endurance, which is in keeping with the high ranking given to organic development as an objective.

Table E.2 Highest ranked pupil effects (compare p. 57)

Rank	Effect	Item
1	Enjoyment of participation in physical activity	16
2	Satisfaction from success in physical activity	29
3	Muscular strength and endurance	2
4	Release from tensions that develop during school day	30
5	General physical development	27
6	Motor co-ordination	14

Table E.3 Lowest ranked pupil effects (compare p. 58)

Rank	Effect	Item
25=	Independent thinking	5
25=	Motivation to achieve in areas other than PE	8
27	Awareness of movement themes	4
28	Remedy physical defects	6
29	Understanding the other's point of view	19
30	Ability to communicate through movement	11

Influencing factors

Tables E.4 and E.5 show the ranking of the highest and lowest items in Part III, question 23 (see pp. 83–4).

The ranking is very similar to that of the state school teachers except that the attitude of school staff to physical education comes very high—rank 2—in independent schools. This may be because the concept of physical education

Table E.4   Highest ranked influences (compare p. 28)

Rank	Influence	Item
1	Adequacy of facilities available for PE	6
2	Attitude of school staff to PE	5
3	Freedom to experiment with different instructional approaches	8
4	Diversity of curricular activities	4
5	Timetable allocation given to PE	19
6	Amount of money allotted to PE for equipment	16

Table E.5   Lowest ranked influences (compare p. 28)

Rank	Influence	Item
15	A considerable proportion of pupils hostile to 'school'	11
16	Problem of 'discipline' in the special PE situation	17
17	Legal liability for accidents	12
18	Total number of different pupils who have to be taught	13
19	'Intellectually inferior' label sometimes associated with PE	14
20	Difficulty for some pupils in providing the required equipment	15

which embraces games is a fairly recent phenomenon in many independent schools and the college-trained professional physical education teacher may meet resistance to change.

Teacher characteristics

Tables E.6 and E.7 list the personal qualities considered most important and least important for successful physical education teaching, from the list in Part III, question 24 (see pp. 85–6).

Table E.6   Highest ranked teacher characteristics (compare p. 31)

Rank	Characteristic	Item
1	Ability to gain respect and confidence of pupils with whom the teacher deals	12
2	Being able to communicate ideas	1
3	Ability to inspire confidence	15
4	Administrative ability	19
5	A thorough knowledge of the subject-matter	3
6	Ability to get on well with colleagues	14

Table E.7 Lowest ranked teacher characteristics (compare p. 32)

Rank	Characteristic	Item
19	A capacity for meticulous attention to details	4
20	Extroverted personality	5
21	A broad cultural knowledge	18
22	A desire to improve world or society in some way	9
23	A good academic record	20
24	A family background in teaching	17

Teaching styles

Table E.8 shows the ranking of the five teaching styles in Part III, question 16 (see pp. 77–8).

Table E.8 Ranking of teaching styles (compare p. 47)

Rank	Teaching style	Mean
1	Direct	3·86
2	Guided discovery	3·22
3	Problem-solving	3·11
4	Individualised programmes	2·88
5	Creative	2·34

Approaches to gymnastics

Table E.9 shows the ranking of the five approaches to the teaching of gymnastics in Part III, question 17 (see pp. 78–9).

Table E.9 Ranking of approaches to the teaching of gymnastics (compare p. 49)

Rank	Teaching approach	Mean
1	Lead-up stages	4·30
2	Movement 'principles'	3·71
3	Physiological 'principles'	3·62
4	Learning 'principles'	3·61
5	Principles of mechanics	3·31

Biographical profile (returns from 38 teachers)

Age

The average age of physical education teachers in the sample was approximately thirty. The age distribution is shown in Table E.10.

Table E.10   Age of teachers

Age group	No. of teachers
21–22	1
23–25	9
26–30	11
31–39	9
40 & over	8

Marital Status
The details are given in Table E.11.

Table E.11 Marital status of teachers

Status	No. of teachers
Single	12
Married without children	7
Married with child(ren)	17

Type of school last attended as a pupil
The distribution is shown in Table E.12.

Table E.12   Type of school last attended

Type of school	No. of teachers
Grammar, direct grant	4
Grammar, maintained	21
Independent	8
Secondary modern	2
School outside Britain	3

A level qualifications
These are shown in Table E.13.

Table E.13   A level qualifications

No. of A levels	Teachers
3	20%
2	50%
1	20%
0	10%

There was a roughly even spread between arts subjects and science subjects.

Length of teaching service in independent schools
The comparative data are given in Table E.14.

Table E.14   Length of teaching service in independent schools

Service	Teachers
Less than 1 year	11%
1–3 years	23%
4–6	25%
7–9	16%
10–12	5%
13–15	5%
Over 15	15%

Plans for further qualifications
Approximately 50% had no plans. Of the others the distribution was as illustrated in Table E.15.

Table E.15   Plans for further qualifications

Projected qualifications	Teachers
B.Ed.	24%
B.A./B.Sc.	20%
Advanced diploma in a specialisation	17%
M.A./M.Phil., etc.	17%
Ph.D.	20%

Teaching of subjects other than physical education
Approximately 95% of teachers reported that they were regularly teaching one or more subjects in addition to physical education.

Previous full-time employment
Table E.16 indicates the extent to which independent school teachers in the sample had been involved in another profession or occupation prior to becoming a teacher.

Table E.16   Previous employment

Previous employment	No. of teachers
None	24
Less than 1 year	5
1–5 years	7
6–10	1
Over 10	1

Graduates
Approximately 25% of the respondents were graduates (including four B.Eds).

Specialist qualifications
These are shown in Table E.17.

Table E.17   Specialist qualifications

Qualifications	Teachers
Third-year supplementary course	10%
Three-year continuous course	70%
One-year course for graduates	5%

*   *   *

Three ex-army and navy qualified men returned the questionnaire.

Although ex-PT instructors still play an important role in many schools, very few answered the questionnaire and the picture that emerged showed that, at least in the larger public schools, physical education departments are run by trained teachers.